Making costume dolls

Making costume dolls

Jean Greenhowe

B T Batsford Limited   London

Watson-Guptill Publications   New York

© Jean Greenhowe 1972
First published 1972
ISBN 0 7134 2313 7

Library of Congress Cataloging in Publication Data
Greenhowe, Jean
Making costume dolls

SUMMARY Discusses the necessary tools, materials,
and techniques for making figures from pipe cleaners
and dressing them in various costumes.
Bibliography: p.
1 Dollmaking — Juvenile literature. 2 Pipe
cleaner craft — Juvenile literature. [1 Dollmaking.
2 Pipe cleaner craft] I Title.
TT175.G74 1973   745.59'22   72–7394
ISBN 0–8230–2987–5

Filmset in Monophoto Century Schoolbook (227)
in 9 on 11 point by
Filmtype Services Limited, Scarborough
Printed in Great Britain by
The Anchor Press Limited, Tiptree, Essex
Bound by William Brendon Limited, Tiptree, Essex
for the publishers
B T Batsford Limited
4 Fitzhardinge Street, London W1H 0AH and
Watson-Guptill Publications
165 West 46 Street, New York, NY 10036

To Mum and Dad

Contents

Introduction

The following pages show how to make and clothe model figures, using glue and all sorts of materials which can be found in most homes.

Full instructions are given for making twenty-six figures complete with their accessories. All the models, which are between 200 mm and 230 mm (8 in. and 9 in.) high, have been made with careful attention to detail, so that they are as authentic in appearance as possible. No sewing skill is needed for making the figures and I hope that this will give them a very wide appeal.

General instructions and ideas about materials are given at the beginning, followed by a section on the method of making the basic figures. For the historical (and prehistoric) costume models, there are instructions for making a man and woman from each period chosen. I have also included a child in the Victorian family to show how to construct a smaller figure.

Imaginative, fairy tale and circus figures follow. Besides being great fun to make, they could be used as illustrations when telling stories to young children. A story would become much more interesting if actual models of the characters could be produced, and it should be possible to illustrate any favourite fairy tale in this way, adapting patterns given for the historical costume figures.

The Western saloon characters come next and I particularly enjoyed making the cowboys. Cowboy clothing and the reasons for its wear make a fascinating study in themselves. For anyone interested, some books are listed in the bibliography. Although most of them are either out of print or unobtainable in this country, public libraries may have copies or be willing to get them on request. Instructions are given for making six Western characters and then ideas on making the other figures in the saloon by adapting the pattern pieces. The saloon layout, scene of many dramatic showdowns in Western films, is designed to show how realistic a group of figures can look when arranged in an appropriate setting. I hope that this may encourage the construction of other settings, perhaps a cave for the prehistoric people, or a treasure island invaded by a band of pirates.

J G

7

General instructions

Note It is important to read through *all* the general instructions and the list of materials before starting to make any of the figures.

Patterns

The patterns are given more or less alongside the making instructions for each pair of figures; except for the Western patterns, these are grouped together because some of them are used for several figures. All patterns are given actual size: they should be traced on to thin paper and all markings copied on to the traced patterns. After cutting out, the paper patterns should be tried against the figure and adjustments can be made at this stage if necessary. Lengthening or shortening of patterns should be done on the lower edges. Some pattern pieces are marked along one edge—*place to a fold in the fabric*—these should be cut from double fabric, placing the edge indicated against the fold to give the full-sized garment. All the traced paper patterns can be kept in marked envelopes and stored in a box.

Cutting out

When cutting out, patterns should always be placed on the materials the same way up as they are printed in the book; this is important for pieces which are not symmetrically shaped. Patterns should be pinned on to the right side of the fabrics; when cutting out leather and other materials which cannot easily be pinned, cut the pattern from thin card, place it on the material, draw round the shape, and then cut out. When cutting

two pieces from a pattern which is not symmetrical, the pattern has to be turned over to cut out the second piece in order to make the pair; this is always mentioned in the instructions. The cut edges of leather pieces are often lighter in colour than the rest of the leather and they can be darkened by colouring with felt-tipped pen. This will greatly improve the finished appearance of the figure.

Gluing

An impact adhesive which glues surfaces together instantly should be used for making the figures. *UHU* glue is very good because it can be rolled off the fingers fairly easily if they become sticky. This type of glue has a tendency to pull into 'threads' when the tube is lifted away from the surface being glued, and care must be taken not to get the glue on fabrics where it is not required. The large size (00) tube of *UHU* comes complete with a screw-on plastic nozzle and this makes spreading small amounts of glue quite easy. When gluing tiny pieces in position, very small amount can be applied with the point of a darning needle or pin. Sometimes a preliminary coat of glue may be necessary before joining non-porous materials such as metal. To save putting the cap back on the tube every time the glue is used and also to prevent leaking, stand the tube upright in an old mug or tumbler. All the clothing is glued directly on to the figures and the raw edges of garments which would normally be sewn together are spread with glue and overlapped about 3 mm ($\frac{1}{8}$ in.). Some pieces are glued edge to edge and this is always indicated in the instructions.

Materials and colours

A brief description of what each figure is wearing is given before the making instructions. When particular fabrics and colours are mentioned, this is for historical accuracy because they were worn at that period. Other materials more suited to the small scale of the figures are often used in the actual instructions and alternative colours and fabrics given.

Adjusting the shape of the figure

If the basic figure shape is not quite right, as the clothing is being glued on extra bits of wadding can be pushed inside the garments with a thin knitting needle where necessary. Small balls of wadding should be pushed inside the clothing at the elbows and knees: this will give shape to the joints when the figure is posed with bent arms or legs.

Faces and hair

A wooden ball is used for the head of each figure. Using the diagram given as a guide for each figure, the faces should be drawn lightly on to the wooden ball with a pencil before colouring. The faces can be coloured with felt-tipped pens or coloured pencils. For the hair and beards embroidery thread and knitting wool in suitable colours are used. For smooth shiny hair use embroidery thread, and for rougher curly hair use knitting wool. Strands of both yarns should be combed or brushed out to tease into finer strands before gluing onto the heads.

Hats

To stiffen and shape a hat made from felt, wet it with a strong solution of starch (the kind used for starching clothes), smooth the hat into the required shape and leave to dry.

Bending and posing the figures

Because wire pipe cleaners are used in their basic construction, the figures are flexible and can be bent into different positions. All female figures with full length skirts have instructions for making a cardboard 'stand' to put the legs into. Many of the other figures will stand without support if carefully balanced, but some are inclined to be top heavy. These figures can be fixed on to a small block of soft wood for a 'stand' by pushing small pins through the edges of the feet, boots or shoes and into the wood. For the saloon floor a piece of insulation board is used into which pins can be pushed easily and this is perhaps the best material to use for a base if many figures are to be displayed. Figures can also be seated or leaned against 'furniture' and these do not require any other support.

Materials to collect

Note Because the pieces of materials used for the garments are so small and varied, a 'materials required' list is not given for individual figures. All the materials are mentioned as each item is made, and the instructions should be read before starting each garment. Since most of the materials used are the 'collect and save up' kind, all sorts of things can be useful. Jumble sales are ideal places to hunt for old 'junk' jewellery, leather gloves, etc. Friends and relatives may help by donating discarded items of clothing, odd balls of wool, dressmaking cuttings, bits of lace and trimmings and perhaps a real fur garment. Although the following list is by no means complete it will give some indication of the kind of materials used throughout the book. It is a good idea to keep different kinds of materials in separate boxes.

Beads and junk jewellery of all kinds, especially very tiny beads which are useful for 'buttons'; sequins; sparkling stones taken from brooches etc; bits of gold chain.

Cake decorations, the edible kind such as 'hundreds and thousands' and 'sugar strands' which make good buttons and beads.

Embroidery thread and knitting wool in suitable colours for hair.

Fabrics from the rag-bag, old handkerchiefs and silk scarves; cuttings from old nylon stockings or tights which are used for covering some of the basic figures (they should be the crepe, non-run kind to prevent laddering), knitted fabrics such as thick nylon winter tights make good 'chain mail' when coated with silver paint.

Feathers from wild birds should be picked up and saved, especially small fluffy ones, brightly coloured budgerigar feathers.

Felt can be bought from art or handicraft shops; flesh coloured felt is used for the hands on the figures.

Felt-tipped pens or pencils for colouring the faces etc.

Fur cut off an old garment or gloves, fur fabric can be used as a substitute.

Glue, which should be an impact adhesive such as *UHU*.

Leather, especially from old gloves because it is worn and soft. For the soles of boots and shoes thicker leather such as an old belt is best. Some leather merchants will sell leather cuttings by weight: they are inexpensive and can be softened by twisting, pulling and rubbing. An old chamois leather is very useful and it should be washed in warm soapy water if it is very dirty.

Paints. Enamel paints are sold in small tins for model making; gold and silver are especially useful. Water colour and poster paints can also be used.

Paper and cardboard of all kinds: metal foils and cellophane sweet and chocolate wrappings; embossed papers such as doyleys and the gold and silver strips off birthday cake frills; cardboard from sweet and biscuit cartons; cardboard toilet roll tubes; paper handkerchiefs; brown wrapping paper; old postcards.

Ping-pong balls for making helmets.

Plasticine can be bought in small packets of assorted colours.

Shoe laces can be used for braids and trimmings.

Trimmings, such as bits of lace, cords, string, gift wrapping braids and cords (especially the gold and silver kind) and ribbon.

Tubing, such as the clear plastic eight-sided ballpoint pen tubes for making drinking glasses; clear plastic tubing of various diameters; empty ballpoint pen refill tubes for making cowboy guns.

Wire, especially fuse wire, which can be bought on cards containing three different gauges; wire paper clips.

Wooden dowelling of various diameters can be bought from woodworkers' supplies shops; round and flat wooden 'lolly' sticks should also be saved.

Zip fastener, taken from a discarded garment to make the cowboys' cartridges.

Useful tools

Small pliers for shaping wire and metal pieces.

Metal snips for cutting wire and metal.

Small tweezers are extremely useful when gluing the pieces in position.

Sharp pocket knife for paring wood.

Small sharp scissors for cutting out fabrics, paper, leather, etc.

Small hammer for flattening wire 'buckles'.

Small hacksaw for cutting pieces of wood dowelling.

Sandpaper for shaping wooden pieces.

Materials required for the basic figures

Adhesive UHU glue.

Pipe cleaners for the body, arms and legs. Ten are required for each figure. Bundles can be bought from tobacconists.

Wooden balls measuring 25 mm (1 in.) in diameter with holes already drilled half-way through are used for the heads. A 20 mm ($\frac{3}{4}$ in.) diameter ball is used for the Victorian child's head.

Wadding is used for padding around the pipe cleaners. *Terylene* wadding, which is sold for making bed quilts, is excellent for this purpose because it holds its shape when pulled into strips. Cotton wool can be used as a substitute, but it is not so easy to work with.

Cotton sewing thread such as *Sylko*, is used for winding around the neck and tying on the wadding to keep it in place. Black is used on the basic shape in the photographs so that it can be seen clearly, but white should be used on the actual figures.

Flesh-coloured felt for making the hands.

Old nylon stockings or tights for covering some of the basic figures.

Making the basic figures

To make a man

The figure measures approximately 215 mm (8½ in.) in height before clothing is glued on. For the head, take a wooden ball and make the drilled hole a little wider by scraping it around the side with a penknife. If solid wooden balls are to be used, first drill a 3 mm (⅛ in.) diameter hole half-way into the ball. Squeeze some glue into the hole.

Gather together four full-length pipe cleaners for the body and the legs. Pipe cleaners are about 165 mm (6½ in.) long. In addition, cut four more to 125 mm (5 in.) for the arms. Spread glue on to the ends and push them all into the hole in the ball. Add 65 mm (2½ in.) extra length on to the 'leg' pipe cleaners by twisting another cleaner, bent double, on to each pair, as shown in *figure 1a*. Make the neck by winding sewing thread around the bunch of cleaners to cover about 6 mm (¼ in.) just below the head (see *figure 1b*). Stick the thread end in place with a dab of glue.

Twist the 'arm' pipe cleaners together in pairs. Twist the four remaining ones together for about 65 mm (2½ in.) to form the body. Then divide them into pairs and twist them together for the legs. Turn up 19 mm (¾ in.) at the end of each leg for the foot; then bend the pipe cleaners into shape at the shoulders and hips as shown in *figure 1b*.

To pad the figure, tear small strips of wadding off the piece and, beginning with the chest and shoulders, wrap it around the pipe cleaners. Wind sewing thread around the wadding as shown in *figure 2a*, to keep it in place and to shape the figure. Use dabs of glue to hold the sewing thread ends in place. Continue this way, padding the arms, hips and legs, and tapering the wadding to nothing at the ends of the arms and legs as shown in *figure 2a*.

Make the hands using the pattern (1) in *figure 4* on page 17. Cut four hand pieces from flesh-coloured felt. Spread them with glue taking care that they are laid out in pairs when doing this. Press the hand pieces together in pairs at the ends of the arms, enclosing the ends of the pipe cleaners as indicated on the hand pattern. Allow the glue to dry, then make cuts in the hands to form separate fingers as shown on the hand pattern. Snip the sharp corners off the finger tips. *Figure 2b* shows the hands glued in position with one hand cut into fingers.

To make a woman

The figure measures approximately 203 mm (8 in.) in height before clothing is glued on. Follow the instructions given for the man but use 115 mm (4½ in.) long pipe cleaners for the arms, adding only 50 mm (2 in.) extra length on to the 'leg' pipe cleaners. When putting on the wadding, keep the arms and legs fairly slim, make the waist very small and pad out the bosom. Glue on the hands using the small hand pattern (2) in *figure 4*, page 17. See *figure 3a*.

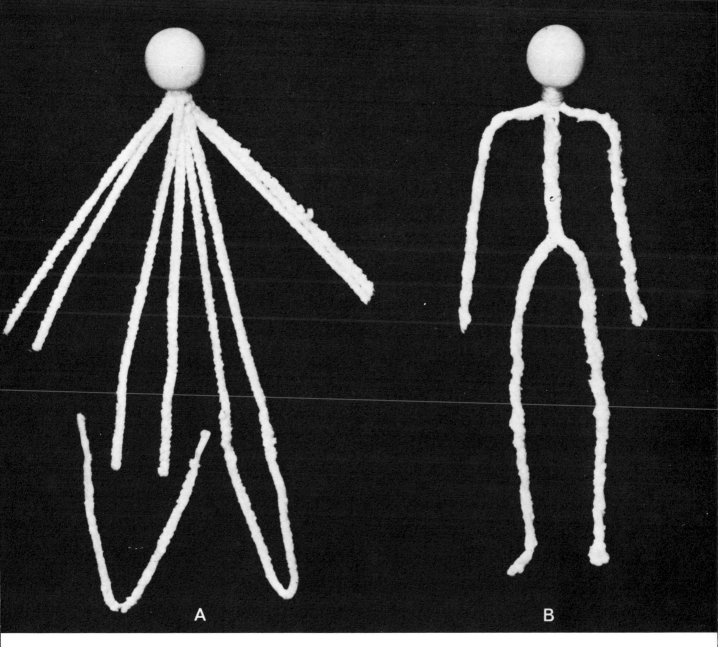

*Figure 1   Construction of basic figure using pipe
cleaners*

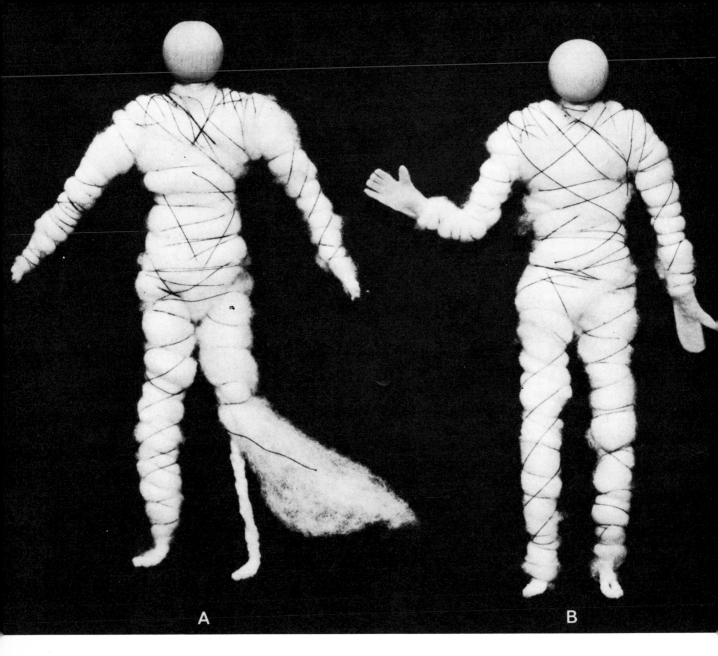

A   B

Figure 2   Padding the basic figure

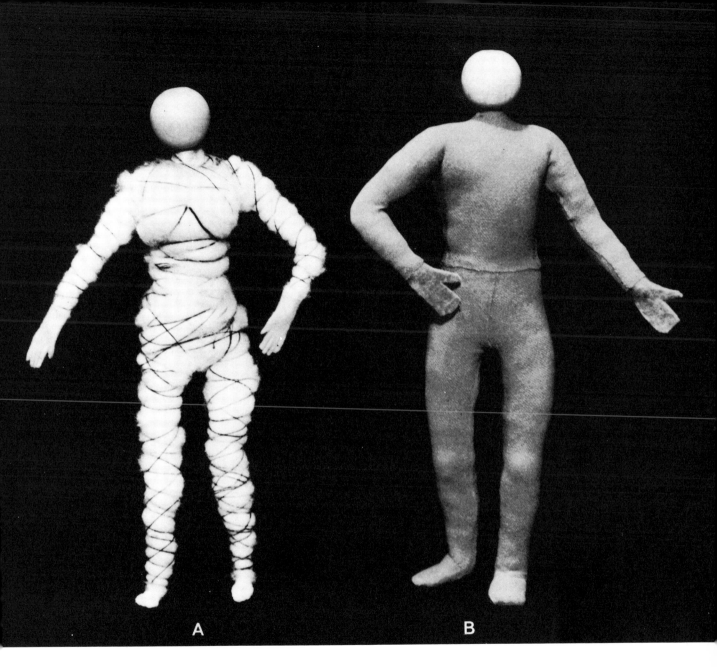

Figure 3a   Female figure

Figure 3b   The nylon covered basic figure

Making the nylon covered basic figure

Note For the figures which are only partly clothed, a fabric covering must be glued over the padding on the basic figures. Pieces cut from old crêpe or non-run nylon stockings or tights are most suitable for this purpose, as this fabric will stretch to fit the shape of the figure. The basic form must be shaped as carefully as possible and extra little pads of wadding should be tied on at the chest, elbows, knees, calves and heels. The colour of the felt used for the hands should match the colour of the nylon as closely as possible, but the felt can be tinted with watercolour paints to get a better match if necessary.

To make a nylon covered man

Make the basic figure and wrap a little wadding around the feet. Cut two leg pieces using the pattern (3) in *figure 4* on page 17. Cut one arms and body piece using the pattern (4) in the same figure. Cut from nylon stocking fabric, taking care to place the arms and body piece against a fold in the fabric before cutting out. Glue one inside leg edge of each leg piece to the inside of each leg, then wrap each piece round and glue the other inside leg edges over the first (note that the toe edges must extend slightly beyond the edges of the feet). Glue the toe edges together and glue the extra length underneath the feet. Overlap and glue the centre edges of the leg pieces at the centre front and back of the figure, then glue the waist edges in position.

Push the head through the small hole cut in the arms and body piece, then glue the edge of the hole to the neck just beneath the head. Overlap and glue the underarm and side edges at the underarms and sides of the figure in the same way as the inside legs were glued. Glue the wrist edges just over the wrist edges of the hands, then glue the waist edges over the waist edges of the legs pieces.

For a smoother finish, glue a second covering over the first.

To make a nylon covered woman

Make in exactly the same way as given for the man, but using the small leg pattern (5), *figure 4* on page 17; and the small arms and body pattern (6) in the same figure.

Figure 4 (opposite)   Pattern for the basic figure (piece numbers 1–6)

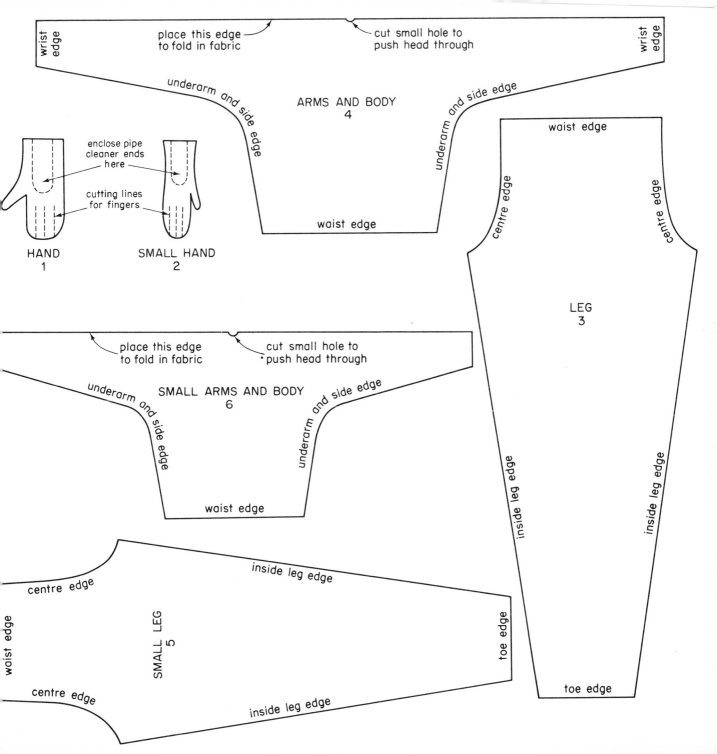

Prehistoric figures—man, woman and baby

The woman

She wears a dark, shaggy fur and carries the baby wrapped in a skin.

Make a nylon covered basic figure using dark tan coloured nylon. Using a needle and brown thread, take four large stitches through the end of each foot to make the toes.

Fur clothing Wrap a piece of fur or fur fabric around the body and glue it in position.

Face and hair Paint the wooden ball to match the body colour. Using *figure 5a* as a guide, colour the cheeks pink and all other markings black. For the hair, glue on strands of black wool which have been brushed to give a rough appearance.

The baby

Only the baby's head is visible above the fur wrapping and a small wooden ball or bead about 20 mm (¾ in.) in diameter is required for this. Colour the ball light brown and using *figure 5b* as a guide, colour the cheeks and mouth pink and all other lines black. For the hair glue on short strands of black wool. Glue the head to the edge of a small piece of fur or fur fabric. Wrap the fur around and glue the edges in place as illustrated. Stuff a little wadding inside the piece of fur to pad it out for the baby's body.

The man

He wears a skin around his waist. He is chipping flint to make an axe head.

Make a nylon covered basic figure using dark tan coloured nylon. Make the toes as given for the woman. To give the body a hairy appearance, cut short clippings of hair off a piece of fur, spread glue on the nylon covering and sprinkle the clippings on to the glue.

Face, hair and beard Paint the wooden ball to match the body colour. Using *figure 5c* as a guide, colour the cheeks pink and all other markings black. For the hair and beard, glue on strands of black wool which have been brushed to give a rough appearance. For the nose, glue on a small piece of nylon fabric rolled up into a cone shape.

Fur clothing Glue a piece of fur around the waist.

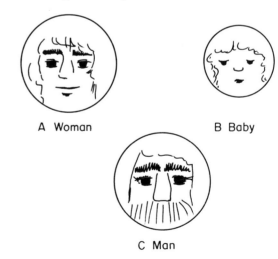

A Woman

B Baby

C Man

Figure 5 Patterns for the faces of the prehistoric figures

Figure 6   Prehistoric figures. Man, woman and baby

Egyptian pharaoh and female attendant of the New Kingdom (1596 to 525 BC)

The attendant

She wears a pale green pleated skirt and shoulder cape of fine linen. On her thick black wig she has a golden fillet or headband and gold ornaments. On top of her wig is placed a cone of scented wax which will slowly melt in the warm atmosphere and bathe her head in sweet perfume. Her collar and bracelets are of coloured beads and gold. She carries a fan made of ostrich feathers and gold. Her face is elaborately made up.

Make the nylon covered basic figure using light brown coloured nylon.

Face   Paint the wooden ball with white water colour. Using *figure 7a* as a guide, colour the cheeks and mouth orange, and the areas above and below the eyes green. Colour the eyes, eyebrows and eyelines black.

Skirt and shoulder cape   These garments are made from a pale green paper tissue to resemble fine linen, white, blue or yellow are also suitable colours. Pull apart the two layers (they are usually two-ply) and use single thickness only. For the skirt, cut a strip 140 mm (5½ in.) wide by 203 mm (8 in.) long. Tightly gather up the strip along its length and gently squeeze and stroke it between the fingers (for the pleated effect); pull open the pleated strip carefully. Several attempts may be necessary to obtain a good result without tearing. Glue one of the 203 mm (8 in.) edges around the figure, just under the bosom, easing the fullness into small pleats, and gluing the 140 mm (5½ in.) edges at the centre back. For the shoulder strap, glue a piece of narrow braid from the centre front, top edge, of the skirt, over the left shoulder and to the top left, back edge of the skirt. Glue a strip of the same braid around the top edge of the skirt. Cut the shoulder cape (piece 1, *figure 9*, page

23) from paper tissue, placing the pattern against a fold in the tissue before cutting out as indicated. Pleat the cape in the same way as the skirt, with the pleats running in the direction indicated on the pattern. Spread a little glue on each front edge and gather up into a small bunch of pleats. Place the cape around the shoulders, overlap and glue the gathered edges at the front of the figure.

A Egyptian attendant

B Pharaoh

Figure 7   Patterns for the faces of the Egyptian figures

Figure 8   Egyptian pharaoh and female attendant of the New Kingdom (1596 to 525 BC)

Collar The collar is made up of small beads, and cake decorations are excellent for this purpose. Use 'sugar strands' for the long beads and 'hundreds and thousands' for the round ones. Cut the collar (piece 2, *figure 9*, page 23) from paper tissue, gluing three layers together for strength. Spread glue on the collar and, using tweezers, stick the beads on in rows, varying the colours and making patterns as illustrated. Glue narrow, gold gift-wrapping braid to the edge of the collar. Place the collar round the neck and glue the centre back edges together at the back.

Bracelets From three layers of tissue glued together, cut out two 6 mm × 25 mm ($\frac{1}{4}$ in. × 1 in.) strips. Glue gold braid and beads on to these strips to match the colours used in the collar. Glue the bracelets around the wrists to cover the join where the hands and arms meet.

Wig Approximately 91·6 cm (1 yard) of black, silky cord of the kind used for anorak drawstrings, is required for the wig. This cord is usually made up of three strands twisted together. First untwist the cord into separate strands, then steam or moisten them to take out the kinks. Cut the cord into 102 mm (4 in.) lengths. Spread glue on to the head and, starting at the face, stick on lengths of cord, taking them from one side of the face, across the forehead and down the other side of the face. Continue in this way, working towards the back of the head until it is completely covered. Now add another layer on top of the first. Trim the wig to an even length all round.

For the fillet, glue a length of gold braid around the head as illustrated, shaping it into a bow at the back of the head. For the gold ornaments, spread glue on two short lengths of gold braid and wind them into small rosettes, gluing a bead in the centre of each one, then glue them to the wig at each side of the face as illustrated.

Perfumed cone Shape the small perfumed cone from a piece of candle wax (it can be made from a coloured candle or a wax crayon). Glue it to the top of the wig.

Fan Cut two base pieces (piece 3, *figure 9*, page 23) from gold card or gold foil glued on to a piece of card. Using a pencil, mark the gold surface of the base pieces to give an 'engraved design' effect. Glue the ends of small fluffy feathers all round the curved edge of one base piece. For the fan handle use a 178 mm (7 in.) length of 2 mm ($\frac{1}{16}$ in.) diameter balsa wood. Colour the handle black, then glue it on to one fan base piece as shown on the pattern. Glue the other base piece to the wrong side of the first base piece enclosing the ends of the feathers and the top of the handle between them. Cut two handle top pieces (piece 4, *figure 9*, page 23) from gold card and glue them one on either side of the handle as shown on the pattern, pressing all the edges together.

The pharaoh

He wears a white linen pleated skirt, tied around the body so that the ends hang down in front. The royal apron and belt worn with the skirt are of gold inlaid with coloured glass and enamels. He wears bracelets and armlets which match the apron. His collar is composed of coloured beads, jewels and gold. On his head he wears the khat *headdress of blue and white striped linen. The royal cobra emblem is attached to a band over the forehead, and the artificial ceremonial beard is held in place by another band attached to the head-band. On his feet he wears gilded leather sandals. He carries a short wooden stick.*

Make the nylon covered basic figure using dark tan coloured nylon.

Face Colour the wooden ball to match the body covering. Using *figure 7b*, page 20, as a guide, paint the whites of the eyes white, and all other markings black. Cut two ears from felt which matches the face colour, using the ear markings shown in *figure 7b*. Glue the ears in position as indicated.

Skirt Cut the skirt (piece 5, *figure 9*, page 23) from a

Figure 9 (opposite) Pattern for the Egyptian figures (piece numbers 1–7)

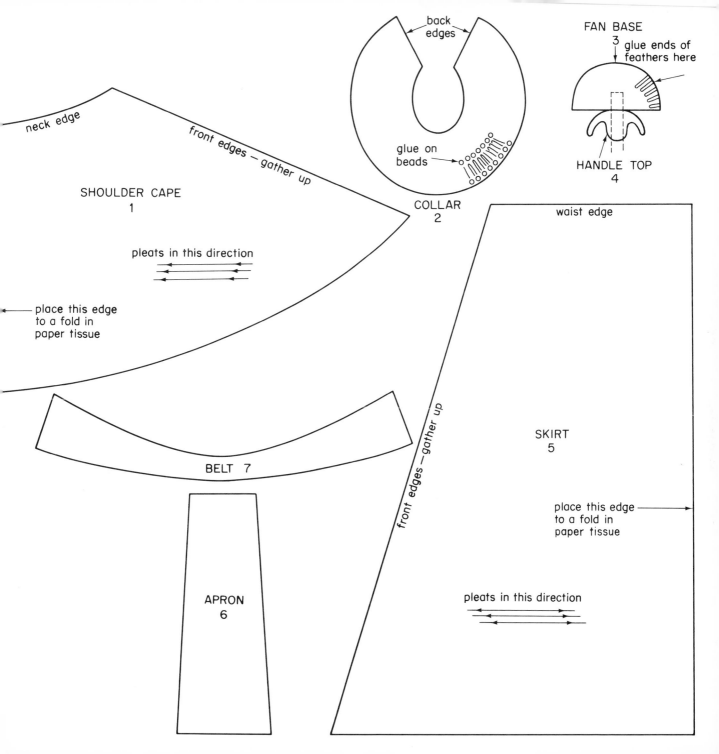

single thickness of white paper tissue placing the pattern against a fold in the tissue before cutting out as indicated. Pleat the skirt in the same way as given for the attendant's skirt, having the pleats in the direction shown on the pattern. Spread a little glue on the front edges and gather up each edge into a small bunch of pleats. Place the skirt around the figure having the waist edge around the waist and glue the gathered edges at the front of the figure. For the front pleated piece which hangs down, cut a long strip 76 mm × 165 mm (3 in. × 6½ in.) from a single thickness of white paper tissue. Pleat the strip along its length, then colour the 76 mm (3 in.) edges as illustrated, for an embroidered effect. Fold the strip lengthways so that one 76 mm (3 in.) edge hangs down 13 mm (½ in.) lower than the other. Gather up the strip at the fold and glue it to the centre front waist edge of the skirt.

Belt and apron   Cut the apron (piece 6, *figure 9*, page 23) and belt (piece 7, *figure 9*, page 23) from thick paper. The inlaid glass and enamel effect is obtained by gluing on pieces cut from coloured cellophane sweet and chocolate wrappings, over gold or silver foil. The gold edgings and ornamentation are cut from embossed gold paper of the kind used for cake frills and doyleys. Cut a few short lengths of narrow ribbon or coloured paper for the 'streamers' at either side of the top of the apron and glue them in position to the back of the apron as illustrated. Glue the top edge of the apron to the centre front of the figure, then glue on the belt, having the short edges meeting at the centre back of the figure.

Bracelets and armlets   Cut 9 mm (⅜ in.) wide strips of thick paper, then glue on cellophane and foil to match the apron. Glue the bracelets and armlets in position as illustrated.

Collar   Cut the large collar (piece 8, *figure 10*, page 25) from paper tissue gluing three layers together for strength. Spread glue on the collar and stick on beads or cake decorations and gold braid as given for the attendant. Place the collar around the neck and glue the centre back edges together at the back of the figure.

Ceremonial beard   Cut a 2 mm ($\frac{1}{16}$ in.) wide strip of black paper for the chin strap and glue it to the face in front of the ears and under the chin as shown in *figure 7b*. The beard is made from a piece of black shoe lace (the tube-like kind which looks as though it is plaited). Cut a 15 mm (⅝ in.) length of shoe lace and push a little wadding inside to pad it out to the shape shown in *figure 7b*. Seal the cut ends by spreading with glue. Glue the beard to the chin strap.

Khat head-dress   A blue and white striped fabric must be used for this, and thin cotton is best. Glue a 152 mm (6 in.) square of this fabric on to another piece of very thin fabric. This will prevent the edges from fraying when the khat is cut out. Cut out the khat (piece 9, *figure 10*, page 25) taking care that the stripes run in the direction shown on the pattern. Make creases in the khat by folding it back along the lines indicated, then cut along the two cutting lines. Plait the three cut edges together tightly, then spread the plait with glue and smooth down all the raw edges and the ends. Glue a little 'knob' of wadding to the top of the head to give shape to the head-dress when it is glued on. Glue the centre front edge of the khat to the forehead and the side pieces behind the ears. Glue the plait to the collar at the back of the figure. Cut the head-band (piece 10, *figure 10*, page 25) and the royal cobra emblem (piece 11, *figure 10*, page 25) from gold card. Glue them in position as shown in *figure 7b*.

Sandals   Cut two soles (piece 12, *figure 10*, page 25) and two straps (piece 13, *figure 10*, page 25) from thin leather. Paint them with gold paint, leave to dry, then glue the soles to the soles of the feet turning up the front points slightly. Glue the straps across the insteps of the feet and to the sides of the soles. Glue the front points of the straps at the position between the first and second toes. Glue scraps of gold embossed paper to the widest part of the straps for decoration.

Stick   Cut a 89 mm (3½ in.) length off a thin round wooden lolly stick, then sandpaper it to taper towards one end. Colour the stick black.

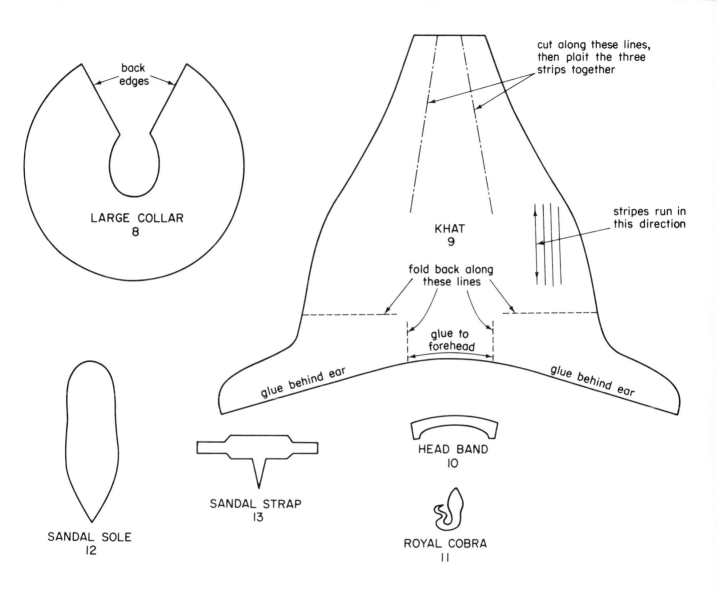

Figure 10 Pattern for the Egyptian figures (piece numbers 8–13)

Roman general and his wife
(first and second centuries AD)

The Roman wife

She wears a white linen Doric chiton, and draped over this a palla of fine emerald green linen. Her hair is dressed in a high chignon at the back with three rows of curls at the front above the face. She wears a necklace of pearls and green stones and a gold bracelet on each wrist.

Make a nylon covered basic figure but cover the top half only, as the legs of this figure are not seen. Make a stand for the figure by gluing a 76 mm (3 in.) piece cut off a cardboard toilet roll's tube on to a 44 mm (1¾ in.) diameter circle of card.

Face Using *figure 11a* as a guide, colour the eyes brown and the cheeks and the mouth pink. Mark all the other face lines with pencil.

Hair Use a skein of red-brown embroidery thread for the hair. Cut the skein right through at both looped ends than divide the thread into two lots. Glue one lot of cut lengths to the back of the head winding them round and round for the 'bun' effect. Make curls with the remaining lengths of thread as follows, cut a few 25 mm (1 in.) lengths of thread and wind them around a ballpoint pen refill tube spread with a little glue, slide the curl carefully off the tube and cut off any excess lengths of thread. Glue the curls to the front of the head in three rows as illustrated, padding the head underneath with more embroidery thread if necessary to raise up the second and third rows of curls.

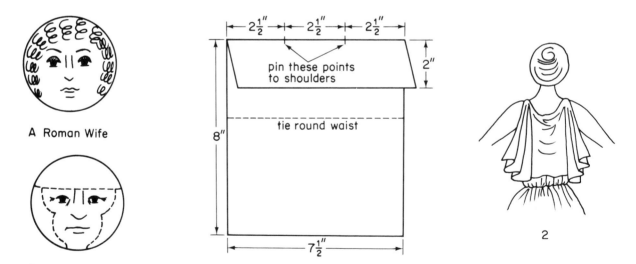

A Roman Wife

C Roman General

pin these points
to shoulders

tie round waist

2½″   2½″   2½″

2″

8″

7½″

1

2

B(1 & 2) Chiton

Figure 11   Patterns for the faces of the Roman figures and for the woman's chiton

Figure 12   Roman general and his wife (first and
second centuries AD)

Doric chiton   Place the legs of the figure in the toilet roll tube stand and stuff wadding around them to make them firm. Cover the stand by cutting a 114 mm (4½ in.) strip of paper tissue and gluing it around the waist of the figure so that the lower edge touches the ground. For the chiton, cut out a 190 mm × 254 mm (7½ in. × 10 in.) rectangle from a man-size white paper tissue, then pull apart the two layers of tissue (they are usually two-ply), one is for the front of the garment and one for the back. Take one piece and fold over 50 mm (2 in.) at one 190 mm (7½ in.) edge to form a rectangle measuring 203 mm × 190 mm (8 in. × 7½ in.). Lightly mark out the 190 mm (7½ in.) folded edge to divide it into three equal portions (see *figure 11b*). Pin the points thus marked to the shoulders of the figure at the back. Check that the garment is long enough to touch the ground. Gather up the paper tissue around the waist at the back and tie a thread around the waist of the figure to hold the tissue in place. Gently crease the tissue into folds at the neck-line and beside the arms as shown in *figure 11b*. Then glue the pinned shoulder points in position. Make and glue on the front piece in exactly the same way as the back.

Bracelets   Use pieces cut from old junk jewelry or very thick wire. Bend into shape and place around the wrists.

Necklace   Thread some tiny white and green beads and tie them around the neck.

Palla   This is made from a strip cut off a fine silk scarf, but any thin soft fabric will do. Cut a 305 mm × 710 mm (12 in. × 28 in.) strip of fabric and drape it around the figure as follows; using pins to hold it in place at this stage, hang one end of the strip over the left shoulder at the front of the figure having the end almost touching the ground, then take the remainder of the strip down across the back to the right side, up across the front to cover the left shoulder and arm, then take a fold of the remaining fabric and drape it over the head towards the right shoulder. If the fabric used is too bulky, cut a narrower strip. Carefully glue the folds in place as necessary and remove the pins.

The Roman general

He wears a white woollen tunic under a cuirass of gilded leather, moulded to fit the body. Strips of red leather hang from the lower and shoulder edges of the cuirass and these are trimmed with gold ornament and fringe. His cloak of terra cotta wool is fastened with a brooch on the right shoulder. On his feet he wears white leather bootees. Relief patterns decorate his bronze helmet, on the crown is a crest of horsehair dyed scarlet. His short sword is carried in a sheath on the left side hanging from a baldrick, slung from the right shoulder.

Make the basic figure. An alternative way of covering the basic figure with nylon stocking fabric is given because only part of the arms and legs are seen. Match the colour of the felt used for the hands as closely as possible to the colour of the nylon fabric.

To cover the arms and legs   Cut two arm pieces (piece 1, *figure 13*, page 29) and two leg pieces (piece 2, *figure 13*, page 29) from nylon stocking fabric. Wrap one arm piece around each arm overlapping and gluing the underarm edges, glue the shoulder and wrist edges in position. Wrap one leg piece around each leg over-lapping and gluing the centre back edges at the backs of the legs, glue the top and ankle edges in position. For a smoother finish, glue on another layer of arm and leg pieces.

Tunic   Cut the tunic (piece 3, *figure 13*, page 29) from white cotton fabric taking care to place the pattern piece against a fold in the fabric before cutting out as indicated on the pattern. Turn in the sleeve and lower edges 3 mm (⅛ in.) and glue them in position. Place the tunic on the figure and overlap and glue the side and underarm edges. Tie a length of thread around the tunic at the waist and space out the folds evenly. Cut a narrow strip of white cotton fabric for the neck scarf and place this around the neck, folding it across at the front and gluing it in position.

Figure 13 (opposite)   Pattern for the Roman figures (piece numbers 1–4)

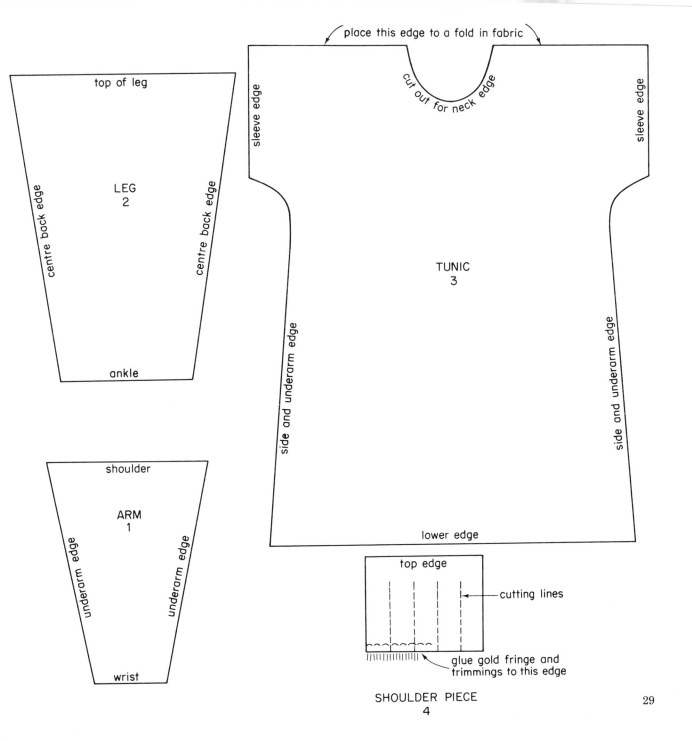

top of leg

LEG
2

centre back edge

centre back edge

ankle

shoulder

ARM
1

underarm edge

underarm edge

wrist

place this edge to a fold in fabric

sleeve edge

cut out for neck edge

sleeve edge

TUNIC
3

side and underarm edge

side and underarm edge

lower edge

top edge

cutting lines

glue gold fringe and
trimmings to this edge

SHOULDER PIECE
4

29

Leather strips Use red leather for these strips or colour a light-coloured piece of leather with a red marker pen or ink. To make the gold fringe edging, cut a 13 mm ($\frac{1}{2}$ in.) wide by 356 mm (14 in.) long strip of cotton fabric and fray about 3 mm ($\frac{1}{8}$ in.) along one long edge. Paint the fringe thus made with gold paint and leave to dry. Cut out the two shoulder pieces (piece 4, *figure 13*, page 29) and glue a strip of gold fringe to the wrong side of the leather at the lower edges so that the fringe hangs down as shown on the pattern. Glue a narrow strip of gold embossed paper, of the kind used on cake frills, to the right side of the lower edge as shown on the pattern. Make cuts at 6 mm ($\frac{1}{4}$ in.) intervals in the shoulder pieces as indicated and glue the top uncut edge of each piece to the shoulders of the figure. Cut out the long skirt piece (piece 5, *figure 14*, page 31), glue gold fringe and paper to the lower edge, then make cuts in the same way as given for the shoulder pieces. Glue the uncut 127 mm (5 in.) edge around the waist. Cut out the short skirt piece (piece 6, *figure 14*, page 31) and decorate and cut it in exactly the same way as the long skirt piece. Glue it around the waist of the figure on top of the long skirt piece.

Cuirass This is made from a bit of leather which should be fairly stiff and firm. Cut out the back piece (piece 7, *figure 14*, page 31) and the front piece (piece 8, *figure 14*, page 31), then using a pencil on the right side of the front piece, impress the chest and hip lines very firmly into the surface of the leather. Using the fingers, carefully mould the leather to shape by stretching and pressing it outwards above the chest lines and above and below the hip lines. Press the leather inwards, then outwards at the abdomen as shown on the pattern. Decorate the front of the cuirass by gluing on pieces of pattern cut from a paper doyley. Glue strips of very narrow braid or string to the neck, armhole and lower edges of the front and back pieces. Paint the right side of both pieces with gold enamel paint and leave to dry. Glue the shoulder and side edges of the back piece to the figure then glue the shoulder and side edges of the front piece in position to overlap the shoulder and side edges of the back piece slightly. Give the cuirass another coat of gold paint if necessary.

Bootees Cut two bootees (piece 9, *figure 15*, page 33) and two scalloped edges (piece 10, *figure 15*, page 33) from soft white leather. Then cut two soles (piece 11, *figure 15*, page 33) from thicker leather. Cut out the centre shapes indicated on the bootee pattern and glue the cut edges together edge to edge to shape the fronts of the bootees. Spread glue on the bootees and place one on each foot joining the centre back edges edge to edge at the backs of the legs. Push small bits of wadding into the bootees at the heels to shape them. Spread glue on the sole pieces and place them on to the bootees pressing the edges of bootees and soles together all round and at the same time push bits of wadding inside the bootees to shape them. Glue the scalloped edging pieces around the top edges of the bootees, then glue a strip of very narrow white braid or string to the top edge of each scalloped piece.

Figure 14 (opposite)   Pattern for the Roman figures (piece numbers 5–8)

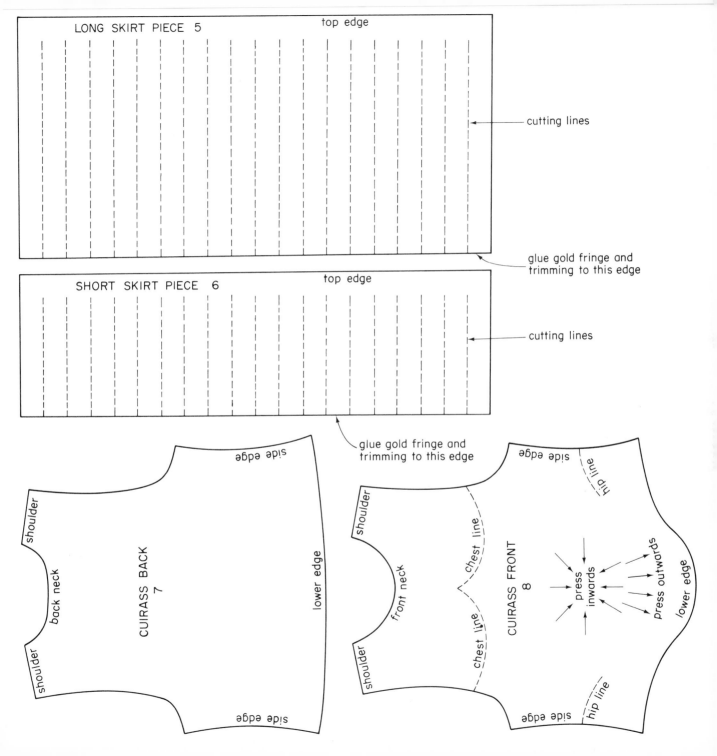

LONG SKIRT PIECE 5 top edge

cutting lines

glue gold fringe and
trimming to this edge

SHORT SKIRT PIECE 6 top edge

cutting lines

glue gold fringe and
trimming to this edge

side edge

shoulder

back neck

CUIRASS BACK
7

lower edge

shoulder

side edge

side edge

shoulder

front neck

CUIRASS FRONT
8

chest line

chest line

hip line

press
inwards

press outwards

lower edge

side edge

hip line

Sword Glue two 6 mm (¼ in.) wide flat wooden lolly sticks together for the sheath, then cut them to the length shown on piece 12, *figure 15*, page 33. Sandpaper the lower edge to the v-shape shown on the pattern. For the sword hilt, cut a 19 mm (¾ in.) length off a thin, round wooden lolly stick. Glue one end of this into half of a wooden bead which measures about 9 mm (⅜ in.) in diameter. Glue the other end of the hilt into a slightly smaller round bead, then glue the hilt to the top of the sheath. (The dotted lines on the sword pattern show the hilt in position.) Paint the entire sword and sheath with gold paint and leave to dry. Cut out eight rectangles from red paper and glue four to each side of the sheath as shown on the pattern. For the baldrick, cut a 3 mm × 229 mm (⅛ in. × 9 in.) strip of red leather, place it over the right shoulder and glue the ends to the top of the sheath at the left side of the figure.

Cloak Use thick tan coloured cotton fabric or very fine wool for the cloak. Cut out 203 mm (8 in.) square of fabric and placing one edge across the back of the figure, glue the two top corners together on the right shoulder as illustrated. Glue the folds of the cloak in position as necessary. Round off the two lower corners, then glue a small gold button to the cloak on the right shoulder for a brooch.

Face Using *figure 11c*, page 26, as a guide, colour the eyes brown and the cheeks pink. Mark all other face lines with pencil.

Helmet This is made from half of a ping-pong ball. Cut the ball in half with scissors using the join line on the ball as a guide. Use one half only for the helmet. Cut the triangular piece (piece 13, *figure 15*, page 33) from thin paper and mark the outline of this on to the outside of the half ping-pong ball, having the lower edge of the paper even with the edge of the half ball as indicated on the pattern. Cut away the marked triangular piece altogether and keep it for use later on for the cheek pieces. Bring together the cut edges of the half ball marked A–B on the pattern to form the helmet shape and hold these edges in position with a piece of sticky tape stuck to the inside. Note that this join will be at the centre back of the helmet and that the remaining cut edges from points B to C will remain open. Cut one cheek piece (piece 14, *figure 15*, page 33) from the triangular piece which was cut away earlier, then reverse the pattern and cut another cheek piece to make a pair. Cut the forehead piece (piece 15, *figure 15*, page 33) and the crest piece (piece 16, *figure 15*, page 33) from thin card. Decorate the helmet, cheek, forehead and crest pieces by gluing on small patterns cut from a paper doyley. To make the red 'horse hair' for the crest, fray out 13 mm (½ in.) along one long edge of a 19 mm × 356 mm (¾ in. × 12 in.) strip of cotton fabric. Fold the strip up several times along its length to make a thick fringe. Then glue the unfrayed edges between the two sides of the crest piece, folding the crest piece back along the lines indicated on the pattern. Assemble the helmet as follows, using the illustration as a guide: glue the forehead piece around the front, then glue the top edge of the cheek pieces to the inside of the helmet, having a 19 mm (¾ in.) space between them at the front. Glue the crest piece to the top of the helmet to cover the opening left there. For the back neck piece cut a 13 mm × 41 mm (½ in. × 1⅝ in.) strip of thin card and glue one long edge of this to the inside of the back edge of the helmet. Curl up the lower long edge of the strip to the outside. Paint the helmet gold and leave to dry. Build up the top of the Roman's head with a lump of *Plasticine* to give it about 13 mm (½ in.) extra height, then put the helmet on the head and adjust the height of the *Plasticine* if necessary to make it fit properly. Glue the helmet in position.

Figure 15 (opposite)   Pattern for the Roman figures (piece numbers 9–16)

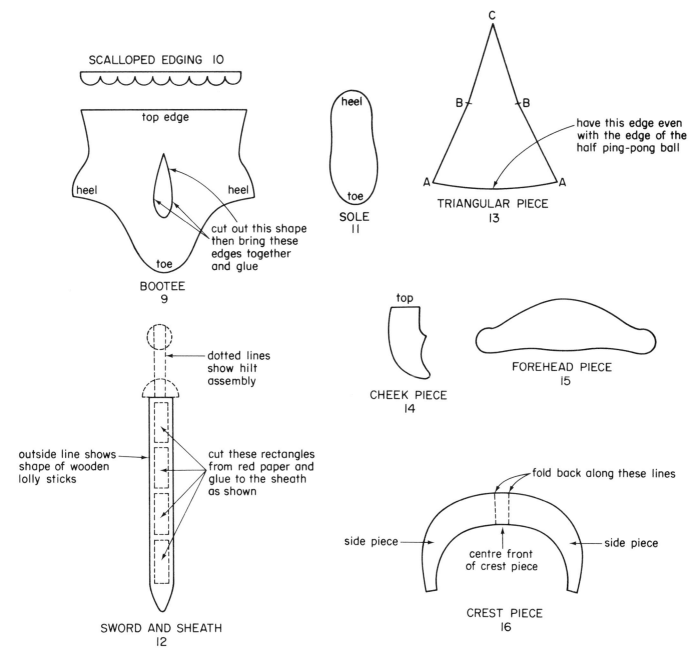

SCALLOPED EDGING 10

top edge

heel

heel

cut out this shape
then bring these
edges together
and glue

toe

BOOTEE
9

heel

toe

SOLE
11

C

B ← → B

A ← → A

have this edge even
with the edge of the
half ping-pong ball

TRIANGULAR PIECE
13

dotted lines
show hilt
assembly

outside line shows
shape of wooden
lolly sticks

cut these rectangles
from red paper and
glue to the sheath
as shown

SWORD AND SHEATH
12

top

CHEEK PIECE
14

FOREHEAD PIECE
15

fold back along these lines

side piece

side piece

centre front
of crest piece

CREST PIECE
16

Viking warrior chieftain and his daughter (ninth to tenth century AD)

The daughter

She wears a red silk kirtle which has long, tight-fitting sleeves and a skirt which trails on the ground. The hem is embroidered with gold thread. Her necklace, belt and beads are of gold and her diadem and bracelet are silver. She carries a horn containing mead.

Make the basic figure. As the legs and feet are not seen they do not need to be clothed. Instead, make a stand by gluing a 76 mm (3 in.) piece cut off a cardboard toilet roll tube on to a 64 mm (2½ in.) diameter circle of stiff cardboard.

Face Using *figure 16a* as a guide, colour the eyes blue and the cheeks and mouth pink. Mark all other face lines with pencil.

Kirtle Use a red silky fabric. Blue and green are also suitable. Cut out two sleeves (piece 1, *figure 18*, page 37) then turn up the wrist edges 3 mm (⅛ in.) to the wrong side of the fabric and glue in place. Overlap and glue the underarm edges of each sleeve wrapping the sleeves around a pencil to do this more easily. Put the sleeves on the arms, pushing them up to form creases until the wrist edges are on the wrists. Cut out two bodice pieces (piece 2, *figure 18*, page 37). Glue one piece to the back of the figure at the shoulders and neck, then glue the armhole edges on top of the armhole edges of the sleeves. Glue the side edges at the sides of the figure. Glue the front bodice to the front of the figure. For the skirt, cut a 140 mm × 229 mm (5½ in. × 9 in.) strip of fabric. Glue a strip of narrow gold trimming or lace painted gold along one 229 mm (9 in.) edge. Using a needle and thread, run a gathering thread along the other 229 mm (9 in.) edge. Place the gathered edge around the waist of the figure to cover the lower raw edges of the bodice, pull up

the gathers and fasten off. Spread out the gathers evenly, then overlap and glue the 140 mm (5½ in.) edges at the back of the figure. Glue the gathered waist edges on to the figure. Place the legs of the figure in the stand and stuff wadding around them to make them firm. Glue the hem of the skirt on to the circle of cardboard.

Belt Cut a patterned strip of gold embossed paper or gold trimming and glue it around the waist to cover the raw edges of the skirt.

Necklace Glue strips of gold braid or trimming around the neck for the necklace.

Beads A length of brass key chain is used for the gold beads but small glass beads can be used as an alternative.

Finger ring Place a small gold ring cut off a chain on to the finger.

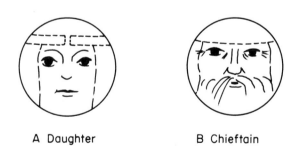

A Daughter   B Chieftain

Figure 16   Patterns for the faces of the Viking figures

Figure 17   Viking warrior chieftain and his daughter
(ninth to tenth century AD)

Bracelet Wind a length of fuse wire around a straight length of thicker wire, then wind the bracelet around the wrist.

Hair Use a skein of pale yellow embroidery thread. Cut the skein right through at both looped ends to make 152 mm (6 in.) cut lengths of thread. Divide the thread into two lots, fold one lot in half and glue the folded loops to the back of the head having the cut ends hanging down the back of the figure. Divide the remaining lengths of thread into two lots, fold them in half and glue the folded loops to the top of the head at each side, having the strands of thread hanging down either side of the face. Comb the threads gently to separate into single strands and smooth them into shape.

Diadem Glue a piece cut off a thin silver bracelet or a length of silver braid around the head as illustrated.

Drinking horn Make the horn from brown *Plasticine*. Roll a small lump of *Plasticine* between the palms of the hands to form a 'sausage' shape about 44 mm (1¾ in.) long with a tapered end. Cut off the broad end of the 'sausage' to neaten it then hollow it out slightly, bending the horn into the curved shape as illustrated. Spread a little glue on the horn to make it shine and leave to dry. Glue gold embossed paper patterns around the rim and to the side of the horn as illustrated.

Figure 18 (opposite) Pattern for the Viking figures (piece numbers 1–5)

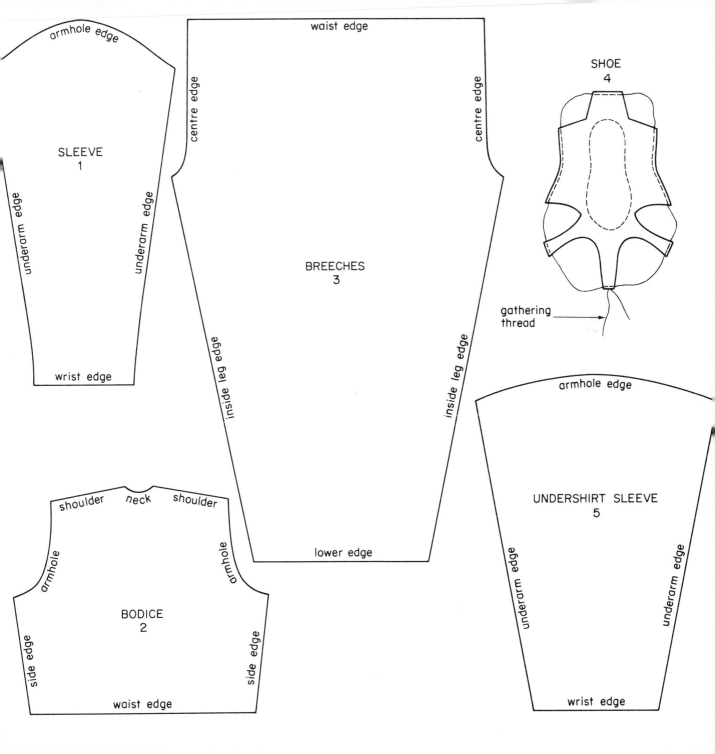

The warrior chieftain

He is dressed for war in a short byrnie or coat of mail over a blue woollen tunic. The legs of his brown woollen breeches are cross-gartered and his shoes are made of soft leather. He wears a cloak made from the skin of a bear which has the paws fastened in front with a brooch. His helmet of gilded metal has horns attached to the sides. He carries a wooden shield covered with leather and studded with bronze ornaments. His scabbard is also leather covered and decorated with gold, as is the sword hilt.

Make the basic figure.

Breeches Cut two breeches pieces (piece 3, *figure 18*, page 37) from brown or blue fabric. Wrap one breeches piece around one leg of the figure taking care that the lower edge covers the heel of the foot, overlap and glue the inside leg edges. Glue the other breeches piece on the other leg in the same way. Overlap and glue the centre edges of the breeches pieces at the centre front and back of the figure; the edges between the legs will not overlap so glue these side by side. Glue the waist edges on to the figure and the lower edges on to the feet creasing the fabric as necessary to fit. For the cross-garters, use very narrow brown braid or strips of leather. Wind them around each leg as illustrated, crossing at the fronts and backs of the legs, then tie the ends of each garter together above each knee.

Shoes Using a piece of old chamois leather for the shoes, cut out two shoe pieces (piece 4, *figure 18*, page 37). Cut two pieces of stiff card for insoles using the dotted line on the shoe pattern as a guide. Glue the insoles to the insides of the shoe pieces. Using a needle and thread, gather up the outer edges of the shoe pieces taking small stitches and beginning and ending at the fronts of the shoes as shown on the pattern. Spread some glue on the cardboard insoles and place a shoe on each foot. Pull up the gathering threads so that the shoes fit the feet and push a little more wadding in at the heels and toes to shape the shoes. Tie the threads tightly around the ankles.

Undershirt Only the sleeves of this garment are necessary as all other parts will be covered later on. Cut two sleeves (piece 5, *figure 18*, page 37) from thin brown cotton fabric then turn the lower edges 3 mm ($\frac{1}{8}$ in.) to the wrong side of the fabric and glue in place. Overlap and glue the underarm edges of each sleeve, wrapping the sleeves around a pencil to do this more easily. Put the sleeves on the arms pushing them up to form creases until the wrist edges are on the wrists; glue the armhole edges to the shoulders and the wrist edges to the wrists.

Tunic Cut two tunic pieces (piece 6, *figure 19*, page 39) and two sleeves (piece 7, *figure 19*, page 39) from thin blue, green or brown fabric. Glue narrow braid, ribbon or trimming to the lower edges of the sleeves and tunic pieces. Overlap and glue the side edges of the tunic pieces, then place the tunic on the figure and overlap and glue the shoulder edges. Overlap and glue the underarm edges of the sleeves, then place the sleeve on the arms and glue the armhole edges on to the armhole edges of the tunic. Cut a strip of narrow silver braid or embossed silver paper for the belt and place it around the waist to take in the fullness of the tunic. Overlap and glue the ends of the belt.

Byrnie The coat of mail is made from a piece cut off the top part of a pair of children's heavy knit winter tights. It can be made from any old garment which is closely knitted in stocking stitch using the purl side as the right side for the 'chain mail' effect. Cut a 152 mm (6 in.) square of the knitted fabric and coat the purl side with silver enamel paint. Leave to dry, then paint with further coats if necessary. Cut two byrnie pieces (piece 8, *figure 19*, page 39) having the rows of knitting in the direction indicated on the pattern. Place one piece at the back of the figure and one at the front, overlap and glue the shoulder edges and then the side edges.

Figure 19 (opposite) Pattern for the Viking figures (piece numbers 6–8)

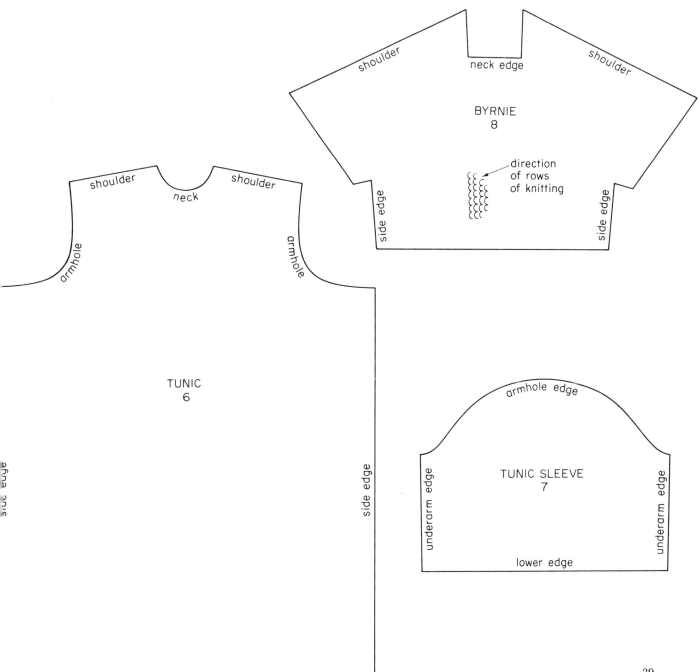

BYRNIE
8

shoulder neck edge shoulder

direction
of rows
of knitting

side edge side edge

shoulder neck shoulder

armhole armhole

TUNIC
6

side edge

side edge

lower edge

TUNIC SLEEVE
7

armhole edge

underarm edge underarm edge

lower edge

Face, hair and beard Using *figure 16b*, page 34, as a guide, colour the eyes blue and the cheeks pink, then mark all other lines with pencil. Use pale yellow knitting wool for the hair and beard. Cut some 50 mm (2 in.) lengths of wool and tease out the ends with a comb; glue the strands to the head all round and to the lower part of the face. Glue the centre of a strand of wool beneath the nose for the moustache. Cut the ends of the hair and beard to even lengths as illustrated.

Cloak The cloak is made from a piece of dark brown fur but fur fabric can be used as a substitute. Cut out the cloak (piece 9, *figure 20*, page 41) taking care that the smooth stroke of the fur is in a downward direction as shown on the pattern. Cut the fur pile quite short around the neck edge and on the paws to make it less bulky. Place the cloak around the neck under the hair and beard and glue the paws side by side to the front of the chest. Glue a small gold button or scrap of jewellery between the paws for a brooch.

Helmet The helmet is made from half of a ping-pong ball. Cut the ball in half with scissors using the join line on the ball as a guide when cutting. Using one half only for the helmet, cut away a quarter of the half ball and bring the cut edges together to form the pointed helmet shape. Hold the cut edges in position by sticking a small piece of sticky tape on the inside. Cut 3 mm ($\frac{1}{8}$ in.) off the lower edge of the helmet. Glue a strip of very narrow braid or leather from the back to the front of the helmet to cover the joined edges. Glue a narrow strip of embossed paper around the lower edge of the helmet. Make the horns from small lumps of cream coloured *Plasticine* by rolling them between the palms of the hands to form 'sausage' shapes tapered at one end. Cut the 'sausages' at the broad ends to make the horns about 25 mm (1 in.) long, bending the horns into shape and glue one to each side of the helmet as illustrated. Glue strips of narrow braid or leather to the helmet around the base of the horns. Paint the helmet gold, leave to dry, then glue it to the head.

Sword For the sword belt, cut a 6 mm × 203 mm ($\frac{1}{4}$ in. × 8 in.) strip of leather. Place it on the figure over the right shoulder, take the ends of the strip to the left side of the figure and overlap and glue the ends at right angles to one another. Cut the sheath (piece 10, *figure 20*, page 41) from leather then cut a flat wooden lolly stick to the size of the dotted shape shown on the sheath pattern. Glue the stick on to the leather sheath, then glue the leather which lies at each side of the stick over the stick to cover it. For the sword hilt, cut a 25 mm (1 in.) piece off a thin round wooden lolly stick, sandpaper it to taper one end, then glue the tapered end inside the top end of the sheath. Glue a strip of thick cord around the top end of the sword hilt for the pommel. Glue a 32 mm ($1\frac{1}{4}$ in.) length of thick cord around the sword hilt above the top of the sheath, folding the length of cord in half and gluing the halves side by side. Glue narrow strips of gold embossed paper to the sheath at the top and bottom. Cut thin strips of leather or use leather thonging and bind it around the sheath in the same way as the breeches were cross-gartered. Paint the sword hilt gold. Glue the sheath to the ends of the sword belt as illustrated.

Shield Cut the shield (piece 11, *figure 20*, page 41) from thick card, then bring the straight edges together as shown on the pattern, holding them in position with a piece of sticky tape on the inside. Cover the shield by gluing on a piece of yellow or red leather, stretching the leather to fit over the convex shape of the shield. Cut the edges of the leather even with the edges of the shield, then cut out the centre circle. Glue three rows of narrow gold gift wrapping braid around the outer edge of the shield. Glue on a gold button or scrap of gold jewelry to cover the centre hole for the centre boss of the shield. Fix gold paper fasteners through the shield at the positions indicated on the pattern. Glue the back of the left hand of the figure into the centre hole in the shield.

Figure 20 (opposite) Pattern for the Viking figures (piece numbers 9–11)

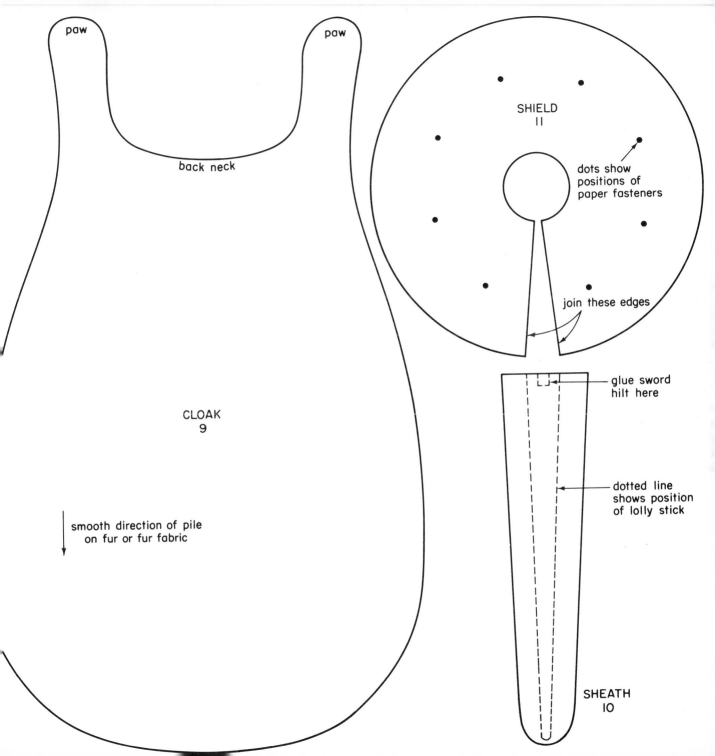

paw

paw

back neck

SHIELD
11

dots show
positions of
paper fasteners

join these edges

CLOAK
9

glue sword
hilt here

dotted line
shows position
of lolly stick

smooth direction of pile
on fur or fur fabric

SHEATH
10

Nobleman and noblewoman of the late Middle Ages (c. 1470)

The noblewoman

She wears a high-waisted gown of cloth of gold. The long skirt trails on the ground and is bordered with orange brocade which matches the belt. The low neckline is edged with a fur collar and the very long, tight fitting sleeves have matching fur cuffs. She lifts her gown and reveals the under-gown of orange velvet which is also seen at the low neckline. On her head she wears a hennin or steeple head-dress of black velvet trimmed with gold braid and this is covered with a veil of pale yellow transparent gauze. A black velvet frontlet frames her face and around her neck she wears a jewelled pendant.

Make the basic figure. As the legs and feet are not seen they do not need to be clothed. Instead, make a stand for the figure by gluing a 76 mm (3 in.) piece cut from a cardboard toilet roll tube on to a 89 mm (3½ in.) diameter circle of stiff cardboard.

Face Using *figure 21a* as a guide, colour the eyes brown and the cheeks and mouth pink. Mark all other face lines with pencil.

Shoulders Cut two shoulder pieces (piece 1, *figure 23*, page 45) from flesh coloured felt. Glue one shoulder piece to the back of the figure, having the neck edge touching the wooden ball. Glue the other shoulder piece to the front of the figure in the same way, lapping it over the back piece as necessary to fit.

Gown and under-gown This is made from gold lurex fabric but silver can also be used. About 1·8 metres of 13 mm (2 yards of ½ in.) wide orange braid or ribbon are also required for trimming the gown. For the skirt, cut a 406 mm (16 in.) diameter circle of fabric. From the centre of this circle cut out a 76 mm (3 in.) diameter

circle. This cut edge forms the waist edge. Glue 13 mm (½ in.) wide orange braid to the outer edge of the circle to cover the raw edges. Using a needle and thread, run a gathering thread around the waist. Put the skirt on the figure with the gathered edge just below the bosom. Pull the gathers up tightly and fasten off. Place the legs of the figure in the stand and stuff wadding around them to make them firm. For the under-gown skirt, cut a piece of orange velvet measuring about 89 mm × 203 mm (3½ in. × 8 in.). Turn in one 203 mm (8 in.) edge 3 mm (⅛ in.) to the wrong side of the fabric and glue in place. Using a needle and thread, run a gathering thread along the other 203 mm (8 in.) edge and glue this to the toilet roll tube at the front so that the lower edge of the velvet trails on the ground. Glue the lower edge on to the cardboard base. Gather up the skirt of the gold gown at the front and glue it in folds and gathers in this position (this is for the hand to hold up when the figure is completed). Arrange the sides and back of the skirt in natural looking folds and glue them in place as shown

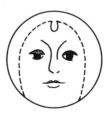 

A Noblewoman   B Nobleman

Figure 22 (opposite) Nobleman and noblewoman of the late Middle Ages (c. 1470)

Figure 21 Patterns for the faces of the Middle Ages figures

in the illustration. Cut two bodice pieces (piece 2, *figure 23*, page 45) from gold fabric, glue them to the back and front of the figure overlapping the side edges at the sides of the figure and having the lower edges covering the raw edges of the skirt at the high waist. Cut two sleeves (piece 3, *figure 23*) from gold fabric. Place a sleeve on each arm and overlap and glue the underarm edges, noting that the lower edges of the sleeves should come well down over the hands. Glue the armhole edges of the sleeves on to the shoulders and the armhole edges of the bodice. Cut a small triangle of orange velvet for the under-gown which shows at the neckline, and glue it in place as shown in the illustration.

Fur collar and cuffs   Real fur, with the pile cut short is best for these but fur fabric can be used as a substitute. Cut out the collar (piece 4, *figure 23*, page 45) and glue it around the shoulders, covering all the raw edges of the bodice, sleeve and under-gown pieces. Cut 3 mm ($\frac{1}{8}$ in.) wide strips of fur for the cuffs and glue them to the lower edges of the sleeves.

Belt   For the belt, cut a strip of braid or ribbon as used on the lower edge of the skirt and glue it around the figure beneath the bosom to cover the lower raw edges of the bodice and the front ends of the fur collar.

Hennin   Cut the hennin (piece 5, *figure 23*, page 45) from thin card and glue this on to the wrong side of a piece of black velvet. Cut out the velvet close to the cardboard shape. Glue strips of narrow gold gift wrapping braid on to the velvet as shown on the pattern. Glue the long straight edges of the hennin together, overlapping them slightly, to form a cone shape. Glue the hennin on to the head.

Veil   A piece cut off a nylon chiffon scarf is most suitable for the veil. Cut a 254 mm (10 in.) square of fabric, then cut a triangular piece off one corner, the base of the triangle measuring about 152 mm (6 in.). Discard the triangle. Glue the 152 mm (6 in.) edge of the piece of fabric to the lower edge of the hennin.

Frontlet   Cut the frontlet (piece 6, *figure 23*, page 45) from two layers of black velvet glued wrong sides together. Glue the frontlet around the face to cover the edge of the hennin as illustrated. Glue a small loop of black thread just beneath the centre front point of the frontlet.

Gold pendant   Glue a piece of gold chain around the neck with a scrap of jewelry beneath it for a pendant.

The nobleman

He wears a green velvet jerkin edged with fur. It has long hanging sleeves which are split open showing the yellow satin lining. The doublet or under tunic of yellow brocade has a high stand-up collar and long tight fitting sleeves. His 'tights' are of yellow cloth and on his feet he wears brown leather shoes with long pointed toes. His shoulder length hair is turned under at the ends and his brown velvet hat is trimmed with a feather.

Make the basic figure, shaping the legs as carefully as possible.

Tights   Use pieces cut from heavyweight nylon stockings or tights having the purl side of the fabric as the outside of the tights. Cut out two tights pieces (piece 7, *figure 23*, page 45). Wrap one tights piece around one leg of the figure and overlap and glue the inside leg edges. Glue the ankle edge to the ankle. Glue the other tights piece on the other leg in the same way. Overlap and glue the centre edges of the tights pieces at the centre front and back of the figure, then glue the waist edges in position.

Shoes   Cut two shoe pieces (piece 8, *figure 23*, page 45) and two soles (piece 9, *figure 23*, page 45) from soft brown leather. Spread glue on the shoe pieces and place them on the feet to cover the ankle edges of the tights, then glue the centre back heel edges together edge to edge at the backs of the feet. Push a little bit of wadding

Figure 23 (opposite)   Pattern for the Middle Ages figures (piece numbers 1–9)

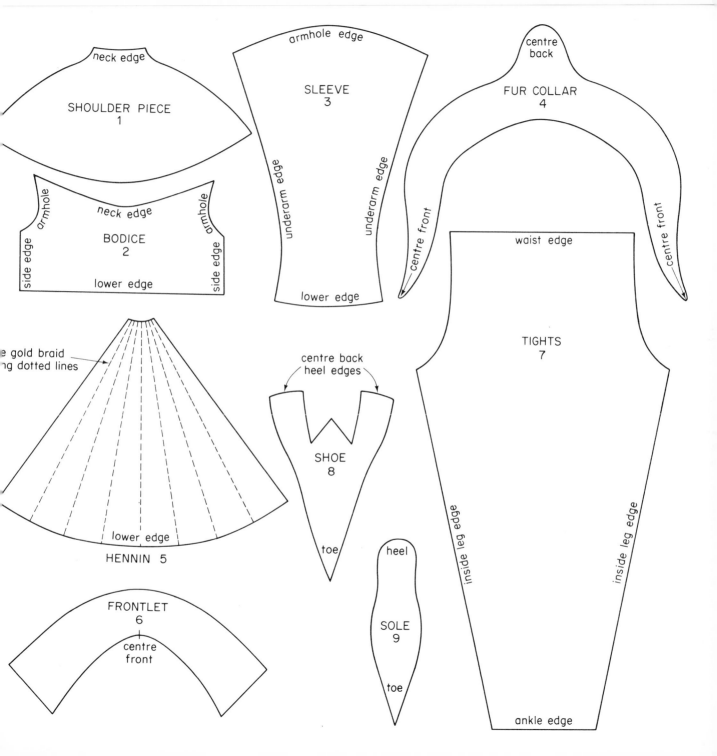

inside the shoes at the heels to shape them. Spread glue on the sole pieces and place the soles on to the shoes, pressing the edges of shoes and soles together all round. Turn up the pointed toes slightly.

Doublet   Only the sleeves and collar of this garment need to be made as the jerkin will cover the other parts. Use brocade or satin fabric in a colour to match the tights. Cut out two sleeves (piece 10, *figure 24*, page 47) then turn the wrist edges 3 mm ($\frac{1}{8}$ in.) to the wrong side of the fabric and glue in place. Place a sleeve on each arm and overlap and glue the underarm edges. Glue the armhole edges on to the shoulders. For the collar, cut a 6 mm × 50 mm ($\frac{1}{4}$ in. × 2 in.) strip from two layers of brocade glued together. Glue the collar around the neck having it standing upright with the short edges just meeting beneath the chin.

Jerkin   This is made from green velvet and the sleeves are lined with satin which is the same colour as the doublet sleeves. Cut two hanging sleeves (piece 11, *figure 24*, page 47) from green velvet and glue them on to a piece of satin having the wrong sides of the fabric together. Cut out the satin close to the velvet sleeves: the satin now forms the sleeve linings. Glue narrow ribbon or braid the same colour as the sleeve linings on to the lower edges of the velvet sleeves. Cut slits in the sleeves as indicated on the pattern. For the fur trimming around the slits use fur or fur fabric cut into 3 mm ($\frac{1}{8}$ in.) wide strips, cutting the fur pile very short. Glue strips of fur trimming on either side of the slits. Overlap and glue the underarm edges of the hanging sleeves. Using a needle and thread, run a gathering thread along the armhole edge of each sleeve as shown on the pattern; pull up the thread tightly and fasten it off. Place a sleeve on each arm and glue the gathered armhole edges on to the shoulders. Cut the jerkin (piece 12, *figure 24*, page 47) from green velvet and glue it on to a piece of thin cotton fabric to act as a stiffener, cut out the cotton close to the velvet jerkin. Glue strips

of fur trimming as used on the hanging sleeves on to the lower edges and around the neck edge. Place the jerkin over the head of the figure and glue the armhole edges over the gathered armhole edges of the hanging sleeves. Using a needle and thread, run a gathering thread across the front and back of the jerkin as shown on the pattern, taking 6 mm ($\frac{1}{4}$ in.) stitches. Pull up the gathers evenly to fit the figure and fasten off. Spread some glue on the waist of the figure and press the doublet back and front on to the glue to hold the gathers in place; overlap and glue the side edges at the sides of the figure. For the belt, cut a 3 mm ($\frac{1}{8}$ in.) wide strip of brown leather and glue it around the waist at the position of the gathering threads.

Face and hair   Using *figure 21b*, page 42, as a guide, colour the cheeks and mouth pink and the eyes and eyebrows brown. Mark all other face lines with pencil. For hair use pale yellow wool. Cut a few 50 mm (2 in.) lengths of wool and spread some glue along one lot of cut edges. Curl these up by winding around a pencil, pull carefully off the pencil then glue the other cut edges to the top of the head. Continue in this way until the head is totally covered.

Hat   For the hat sides, cut a 6 mm × 70 mm ($\frac{1}{4}$ in. × $2\frac{3}{4}$ in.) strip of thin card. Join the strip into a tube by bringing the 6 mm ($\frac{1}{4}$ in.) edges together and holding them in position with a piece of sticky tape. Glue one edge of the tube at right angles on to a piece of thin card, then cut out the card even with the tube. Cover this hat shape by gluing on a piece of brown velvet, stretching and creasing the velvet as necessary to fit the shape. Cut off any excess velvet even with the hat shape. For the hat brim, cut a 6 mm ($\frac{1}{4}$ in.) wide strip of brown velvet about 102 mm (4 in.) in length, spread glue on the wrong side and fold it in half widthways. Glue the strip around the base of the hat and cut off any excess length. Glue the hat to the head, then glue a feather to the back as illustrated.

Figure 24 (opposite)   Pattern for the Middle Ages figures (piece numbers 10–12)

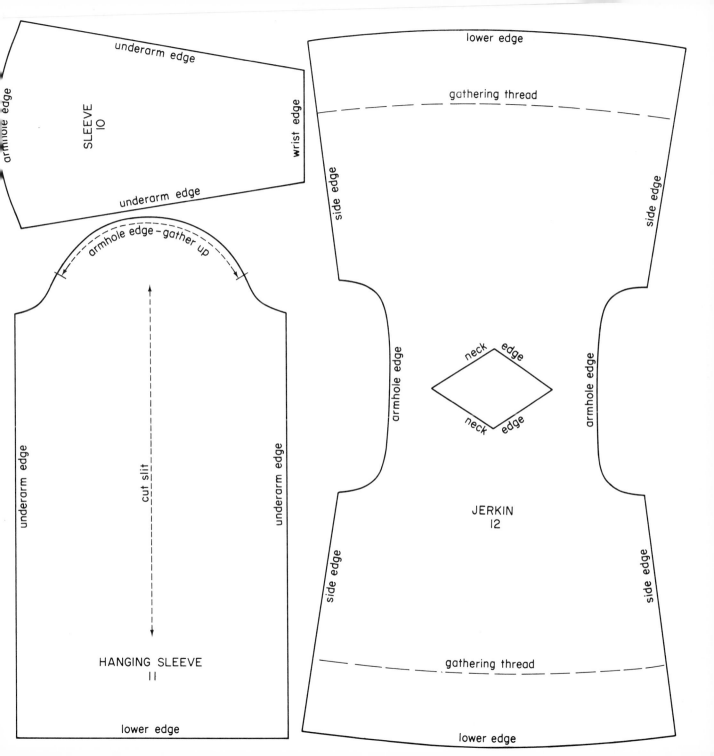

Cavalier and lady (c. 1640)

The lady

She wears a high waisted gown of rich crimson satin, with a white lace collar and cuffs. Her hair is drawn back from the forehead into a flat bun at the back, and the side hair is dressed in ringlets. She carries a black taffeta face mask to protect the complexion when out of doors.

Make the basic figure using the hand and arm piece 1, *figure 27*, page 51, instead of the hand pattern given in the basic instructions. As the legs and feet are not seen on this figure they do not need to be clothed. Instead, make a stand for the figure by gluing a 76 mm (3 in.) piece cut off a cardboard toilet roll tube on to a 89 mm (3½ in.) diameter circle of stiff cardboard.

Shoulders   Cut two shoulder pieces (piece 2, *figure 27*, page 51) from flesh-coloured felt. Glue one shoulder piece to the back of the figure having the neck edge touching the wooden ball. Glue the other piece to the front of the figure in the same way, lapping it over the back piece as necessary to fit.

Face   Using *figure 25a* as a guide, colour the eyes blue, the cheeks and mouth pink and the eyebrows and small forehead curls brown. Mark all other face lines with pencil.

Hair   Use a skein of light brown embroidery thread for the hair. Spread some glue on top of the head, then cut some 64 mm (2½ in.) lengths of the thread; fold the lengths in half and having the folds just above the forehead curls, stick the thread to the top of the head until this part is covered. For the bun, wind some embroidery thread around two fingers, twist the loops thus made into a figure eight, fold the loops together and glue the bun to the head. Fill in the sides by adding ringlets of

varying lengths made as follows: cut a short length of thread, spread some glue along a darning needle near to the point and wind the thread along the needle towards the point to cover the glue, then carefully slide off the ringlet. Wind a piece of narrow braid or cord around the bun, gluing it into a bow shape at one side.

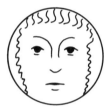

A Lady

B Cavalier

Figure 25   Patterns for the faces of the cavalier figures

Figure 26   Cavalier and lady (c. 1640)

Gown This is made from red satin, but amber, yellow, white, black and blue are also suitable. For the skirt, cut a 178 mm × 457 mm (7 in. × 18 in.) strip of fabric. Overlap and glue the 178 mm (7 in.) edges. Using a needle and thread, run a gathering thread along one long edge. Put the skirt on the figure, having the gathered edge just beneath the bosom. Pull the gathers up and fasten off. Spread out the gathers evenly and glue the gathered raw edges on to the figure. Place the legs of the figure in the stand and stuff wadding around them to make firm. Turn the lower raw edges of the skirt to the inside, pinning them in position, so that the front is left long enough to trail on the ground and the back is left as long as possible to form a train. Crease the turned edges to mark the turning line all round. Remove the pins and glue the turned edges in position. If the skirt stands out rather stiffly it can be softened into folds by spreading glue on the inside where necessary and smoothing into shape. Cut a 25 mm × 102 mm (1 in. × 4 in.) strip of satin for the bodice and glue this around the figure just under the arms and at the top edge of the skirt. Overlap and glue the short raw edges at the back of the figure. For the 'basque skirt' part of the bodice, glue together two layers of satin fabric then cut out the front basque (piece 3, *figure 27*, page 51) and the back basque (piece 4, *figure 27*, page 51). Make cuts in the back basque as indicated on the pattern. Glue thin cord or thread all round the lower and side edges of both basque pieces as illustrated. Glue the high waist edges of the front and back basque pieces in position on the figure, to cover the top raw edges of the skirt. Glue a strip of narrow braid for a belt around the top of the basque pieces. Then glue a bow made from the same braid at the front left side of the belt. Cut two sleeves (piece 5, *figure 27*, page 51) from satin. Overlap and glue the underarm edges of each sleeve. Place the sleeves on the arms and glue the armhole edge of each one just on to the shoulders, creasing the fabric as necessary to fit. Push a little wadding inside each sleeve to pad it out. Then glue the lower edges of each sleeve to the top edges of the arm and hand pieces, creasing the fabric to fit.

Collar Cut the collar (piece 6, *figure 27*, page 51) from thin white fabric, then glue on two rows of 6 mm (¼ in.) wide white lace edging, one to each edge, as shown on the pattern. Ease the lace edging around the curves as it is glued on. Glue the collar around the shoulders, covering all the upper raw edges of the bodice and sleeves. Glue a small button or scrap of jewelry to the centre front of the collar for a brooch.

Cuffs For each cuff, cut two 50 mm (2 in.) strips of narrow, white lace edging. Using a needle and thread, gather the two pieces of lace together, then glue the gathered edges to the lower edge of each sleeve.

Pearls Thread some pearl or white beads and tie them around the neck.

Mask Glue a small piece of black taffeta on to a piece of card. Then cut out the mask (piece 7, *figure 27*, page 51). Glue narrow lace edging to the card side of the mask so that only a very narrow bit shows on the right side of the mask. Glue a length of black sewing thread to each side of the mask.

The cavalier

He is elegantly dressed in doublet and breeches of blue-grey satin. A matching cloak draped over his left shoulder is lined with crimson velvet. His hair is arranged in shoulder-length ringlets with one long love lock brought forward over the left shoulder and tied with red ribbon. Ostrich plumes decorate his wide-brimmed black hat. His leather 'bucket top' boots have 'butterfly' spur leathers attached to the spurs and the ruffled lace tops of his boot hose can be seen inside the boot tops. His baldrick supports a sword with a silver hilt and scabbard. He carries embroidered leather gauntlets.

Make the basic figure.

Note 1·8 metres (2 yards) of very narrow lace edging are required for the silver trimming on the doublet,

Figure 27 (opposite) Pattern for the cavalier figures (piece numbers 1–8)

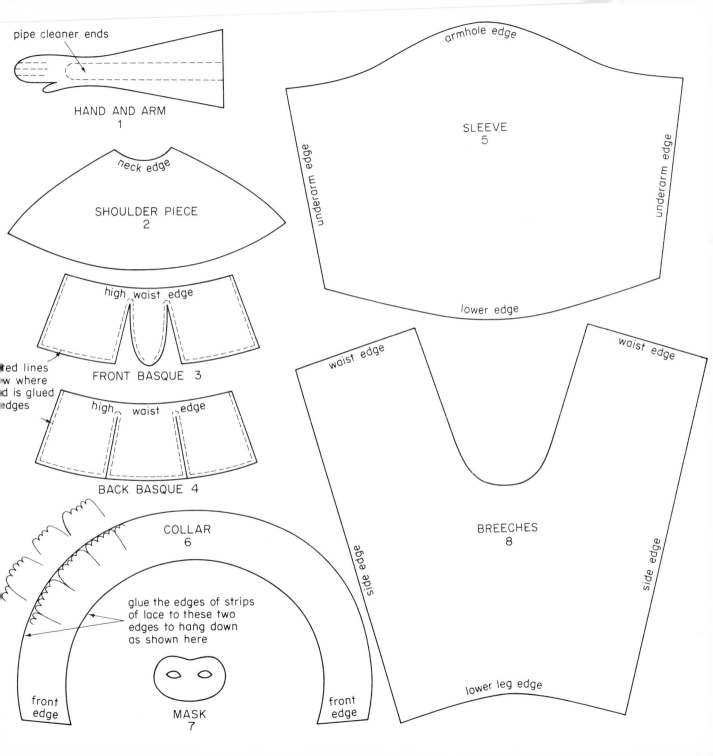

pipe cleaner ends

HAND AND ARM
1

neck edge

SHOULDER PIECE
2

high waist edge

FRONT BASQUE 3

...ed lines
...w where
...d is glued
...dges

high waist edge

BACK BASQUE 4

COLLAR
6

glue the edges of strips
of lace to these two
edges to hang down
as shown here

front edge

MASK
7

front edge

SLEEVE
5

armhole edge

underarm edge

underarm edge

lower edge

waist edge

waist edge

side edge

side edge

BREECHES
8

lower leg edge

breeches and cloak. Paint the lace with silver enamel and leave to dry. About 0·9 metres (1 yard) of narrow white lace edging is also required for the lace tops of the boot hose. Blue-grey satin is used for the doublet, breeches and cloak. Dark brown, black, fawn and green are also suitable colours.

Breeches Cut two breeches pieces (piece 8, *figure 27*, page 51) from satin. Wrap one breeches piece around one leg and overlap and glue the side edges at the outside leg of the figure; glue the other breeches piece on the other leg in the same way. Overlap and glue the centre edges of the breeches pieces at the centre front and back of the figure; the edges between the legs will not overlap, so glue these side by side. Glue the waist edge to the figure. Glue a strip of 6 mm (¼ in.) wide red ribbon or fabric down each side of the breeches to cover the glued overlaps, then glue two strips of narrow silver lace edging side by side over the red ribbon at each side. Glue strips of narrow red braid, trimming or fringe to the lower edges of the breeches.

Doublet and undershirt For the undershirt sleeves cut two sleeves (piece 9, *figure 28*, page 53) from white cotton fabric, ignoring the reference to lace and ribbon trimming on the pattern. Place the sleeves on the arms, overlap and glue the underarm edges. Glue the armhole edges to the shoulders of the figure, creasing them as necessary to take up the fullness. Glue the wrist edges to the wrists in the same way. Cut the two doublet sleeves (piece 9, *figure 28*, page 53) from satin. Glue strips of red ribbon and silver lace edging on the sleeves from the wrist to the armhole edges as shown on the pattern, to match the breeches trimming. Take care to make a right and left sleeve when doing this because the trimming is off centre. Cut the sleeves along the cutting lines between the two strips of lace edging. Place the sleeves over the undershirt sleeves having the lace trimming towards the front of the figure then glue the underarm, armhole and wrist edges in position as given for the undershirt sleeves. Cut the two doublet pieces (piece 10, *figure 28*, page 53) from satin. Turn lower edges 6 mm (¼ in.) to the wrong side of the fabric and glue in place. Glue a strip of red ribbon and two strips of silver lace down the centre front of one of the doublet pieces as shown on the pattern, then make a cut between the two strips of lace from the lower edge upwards as indicated on the pattern. Place the doublet back piece on the figure and glue it to the shoulders. Place the doublet front on the front of the figure and glue the shoulder edges over the shoulder edges of the back piece. Glue the armhole edges of the doublet pieces over the armhole edges of the sleeves. Overlap and glue the side edges at the sides of the figure.

Lace edged collar and cuffs Cut the collar (piece 11, *figure 28*, page 53) from white cotton fabric, then glue narrow white lace edging to the front and outer edges. Glue the neck edge of the collar to the neck of the figure. For each cuff, cut a 6 mm (¼ in.) wide strip of white cotton fabric long enough to go around each wrist. Glue narrow white lace edging to one edge of each cuff piece, then glue the cuffs over the wrist edges of the sleeves as illustrated.

Figure 28 (opposite)   Pattern for the cavalier figures (piece numbers 9–11)

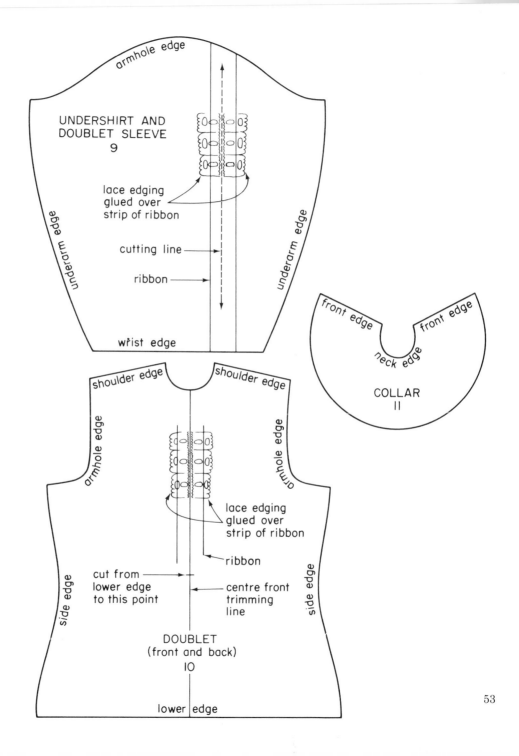

UNDERSHIRT AND
DOUBLET SLEEVE
9

armhole edge

underarm edge

underarm edge

lace edging
glued over
strip of ribbon

cutting line →

ribbon →

wrist edge

COLLAR
11

front edge

front edge

neck edge

shoulder edge

shoulder edge

armhole edge

armhole edge

side edge

side edge

lace edging
glued over
strip of ribbon

ribbon →

cut from →
lower edge
to this point

← centre front
trimming
line

DOUBLET
(front and back)
10

lower edge

Bucket top boots From soft leather cut two boot pieces (piece 12, *figure 29*, page 55) then, using patterns given on page 92 for the Western saloon figures, cut two soles (piece 5, *figure 56*) and two of each of the heel pieces (piece 6, *figure 56*) from thicker leather. Stick together the boots, soles and heels in the same way given for the old timer on page 84. Turn down the wide boot tops until they reach the feet, then turn them part of the way back up again, leaving a fold to form the bucket tops.

Spurs Make and glue on the back metal parts of the spurs in exactly the same way as given for the young ranch hand (*figure 55*, page 90). Cut two butterfly spur leathers (piece 13, *figure 29*, page 55) from the same soft leather as used for the boots. Glue the centres of the spur leathers to the fronts of the boots as illustrated. Cut four 25 mm (1 in.) long, thin strips of leather, then on each boot, glue one strip under the instep and up the sides of the boot to meet the ends of the spur. Glue another strip across the butterfly spur leather to meet the ends of the spur.

Boot hose tops For each leg cut a strip of narrow white lace edging about 457 mm (18 in.) in length. Using a needle and thread, run a gathering thread along one edge of each length of lace. Pull up the gathers. Spread some glue on the legs just below the lower edges of the breeches and press the gathered edges of the lace on to the glue. Tuck the lace in to the bucket tops of the boots using a little glue to hold them in position.

Face, hair and beard Using *figure 25b*, page 48, as a guide, mark the features lightly on to the head with pencil. Use dark brown embroidery thread for the hair and beard. For the beard cut short lengths, spread them with glue and press them on to the face, shaping them into a pointed 'Vandyke' beard. Glue on short lengths of thread for the moustache. To make the ringlets for the hair, cut a few 50 mm (2 in.) lengths of thread, spread one lot of ends with a little glue and wind carefully around a thin knitting needle to form a curl. Slide the curl carefully off the needle and glue the straight ends

of the thread to the head. Glue ringlets all round to cover the head. Make the 'love lock' ringlet at the left side of the head extra long and tie a bow of thick thread around it for a ribbon. Glue a few short strands of thread on to the forehead. Colour the eyes brown and the cheeks and mouth pink, mark all other face lines with pencil.

Hat Cut the hat brim (piece 14, *figure 29*, page 55), the hat side piece (piece 15, *figure 29*, page 55) and the flat crown (piece 16, *figure 29*, page 55) from black felt. Glue the short edges of the hat side piece together overlapping slightly. Glue the lower edge of the hat side piece at right angles to the centre hole in the brim, then glue the edge of the flat crown piece at right angles to the top edge of the hat side piece. Glue a narrow strip of silver or silky braid around the base of the side piece for the hat band. For the ostrich plumes use soft white feathers; these can be curled by pulling them firmly between the edge of a blunt knife blade and the thumb. Glue the feathers to the hat and the hat to the head as illustrated.

Baldrick Cut a 240 mm (9½ in.) length of braid or ribbon about 13 mm (½ in.) in width. Fold over 13 mm (½ in.) at one end to form a loop, then tuck the other end of the strip sideways into the loop. Glue the ends of the braid in these positions leaving the loop open to slip the sword in to. Place the baldrick on the right shoulder to hang down at the left side of the figure.

Sword Cut a 114 mm (4½ in.) length of 3 mm (⅛ in.) diameter wooden dowelling. Sandpaper the dowelling so that it tapers towards one end, then flatten the lower 'scabbard' part by rubbing it with sandpaper on either side, leaving the top 19 mm (¾ in.) circular for the sword hilt. Wind a length of 15 amp fuse wire around the hilt to cover it and glue a small bead on to the end of the hilt. Twist together two 152 mm (6 in.) lengths of 15 amp fuse wire, then twist the wire around the hilt for the guard as illustrated. Paint the bead and the wooden scabbard silver. Slide the sword into the baldrick.

Gauntlets Cut two gauntlets (piece 17, *figure 29*, page 55) from thin leather. Then make cuts to divide into fingers as shown on the pattern. Decorate the wrist edges by gluing on strips of thin cord or trimming. Glue the gauntlets to the right hand.

Cloak Make a paper pattern for the cloak as follows: cut out a 240 mm (9½ in.) diameter circle, then cut a 25 mm (1 in.) diameter circle from the centre of the first, for the neck edge. Fold the circle into quarters, then cut away one quarter altogether. Using this three quarter circle as a pattern cut the cloak from satin. Glue the edges of the satin cloak on to a piece of velvet, then cut out the velvet close to the satin edges. Stick silver lace trimming to the edges of the satin side of the cloak. Arrange the neck edge over the left shoulder and arm as illustrated, allowing most of the cloak to hang down the back of the figure in folds. Glue the folds in position.

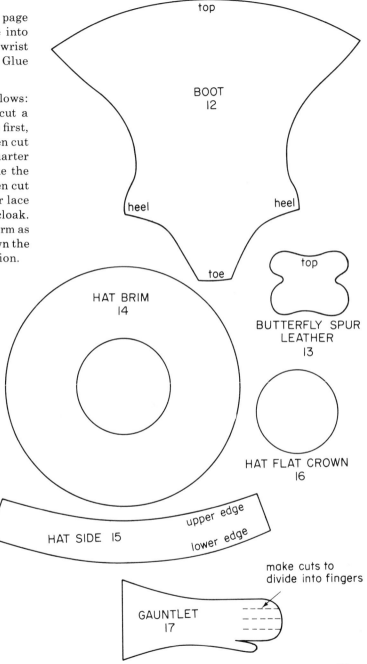

Figure 29 Pattern for the cavalier figures (piece numbers 12–17)

55

Victorian family of the 1850s

The mother

She wears a purple silk dress with a flounced skirt over a crinoline. Her red velvet jacket is edged with pink lace to match the lace trimming on the flounced skirt. Her white lacy bonnet is worn far back on the head and trimmed with flowers and ribbons. The parasol is of lilac silk, matching the large fringed cashmere shawl draped over her arm.

Make the basic figure, using thin, cream or white coloured leather instead of felt for the hands, to give the effect of gloves. Take care to cut the hands in pairs by reversing the pattern for two of the pieces when cutting out. Mark the back of the gloves with three stitching lines (see illustration). As the legs and feet are not seen on this figure they do not need to be clothed. Instead, make a stand for the figure by gluing a 76 mm (3 in.) piece cut off a cardboard toilet roll tube onto a 89 mm (3½ in.) diameter circle of stiff cardboard.

Face and hair Using *figure 30a* as a guide, colour the eyes brown and the cheeks and mouth pink. Mark all other face lines with pencil. For the hair, cut some 102 mm (4 in.) lengths of dark brown embroidery thread. Glue the centre of the lengths to the centre top of the head, then glue the strands down each side of the face and up towards the back of the head.

Crinoline shape Place the legs of the figure in the stand and stuff wadding around them to make firm. For the crinoline shape underneath the dress, cut a 152 mm × 508 mm (6 in. × 20 in.) strip of buckram or some other very stiff material. Using a needle and thread, run a gathering thread along one long edge, put the gathered edge around the waist. Pull up the gathers tightly and fasten off. Overlap and glue the 152 mm (6 in.) edges.

Using the fingers, press the gathered folds of the fabric flat from the waist downwards to give the crinoline a smooth bell shape.

Dress 57 cm of 90 cm (⅝ yard of 36 in.) fabric is required for the dress and about 3·6 metres (4 yards) of 13 mm (½ in.) lace for trimming the dress and jacket. The dress is made from thin purple fabric with a small red check woven in. Other suitable colours are dark red, green or blue. The fabric used should crease easily so that the flounced skirt may be made to drape properly. For the lowest flounce on the skirt, cut a 178 mm × 762 mm (7 in. × 30 in.) strip of fabric, fold it in half widthways and iron the fold. Glue lace trimming to the strip about 13 mm (½ in.) up from the fold. Using a needle and thread, run a gathering thread along the strip through both thicknesses of fabric close to the raw edges. Pull up the gathers tightly and pinch and press the strip into pleats with the fingers. Loosen the gathers and place the strip over the crinoline shape having the folded edge touching the floor. Space out the gathers all round and fasten off the gathering thread.

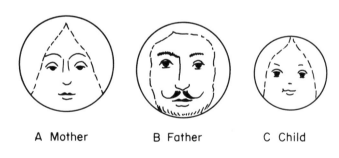

A Mother   B Father   C Child

Figure 30 Patterns for the faces of the Victorian figures

Figure 31   Victorian family of the 1850s

Overlap and glue the short edges of the strip, then glue the gathered raw edges to the crinoline. Glue the folds of the flounce to the crinoline shape as necessary to make it hang properly. For the second flounce, cut a 178 mm × 660 mm (7 in. × 26 in.) strip of fabric. For the third flounce, cut a 178 mm × 610 mm (7 in. × 24 in.) strip. Treat these strips in the same way as the first, spacing them at even intervals (see illustration). For the dress bodice, cut a 38 mm (1½ in.) square of the dress fabric and glue this to the front of the figure just beneath the head.

Undersleeves Cut two strips of white lace or lace trimming measuring about 25 mm × 76 mm (1 in. × 3 in.) Overlap and glue the 25 mm (1 in.) edges of each strip. Using a needle and thread, run a gathering thread along the 76 mm (3 in.) edges. Put the sleeves on the arms, having one gathered edge overlapping the wrist edge of each glove. Pull up the gathers and fasten off. Glue the gathered edges in place.

Jacket The jacket is made from dark red velvet, although thin wool could be used as an alternative. Cut two sleeves (piece 1, *figure 32*, page 59) from red velvet and glue gathered lace trimming to the lower edges. Place a sleeve on each arm and overlap and glue the underarm edges. Glue the armhole edges on to the shoulders. Cut out the jacket back (piece 2, *figure 32*, page 59) and glue it to the back of the figure at the shoulder, armhole and side edges. Cut out two jacket fronts (piece 3, *figure 32*, page 59) taking care to reverse the pattern when cutting the second of the pair. Glue the fronts in position at the shoulder and armhole, front and side edges. Cut out the jacket skirt (piece 4, *figure 32*, page 59) and glue the waist edge around the waist of the figure, overlapping the lower edges of the jacket fronts and back slightly. Glue gathered lace trimming to the centre fronts, lower edges and back neck edge of the jacket. Glue a small bow of ribbon or braid to the waist at the centre front of the jacket.

Bonnet Glue a piece of white lacy fabric about 102 mm (4 in.) square on to a piece of buckram, then from this, cut out the bonnet back piece (piece 5, *figure 32*, page 59) and the bonnet (piece 6, *figure 32*, page 59). Glue the back edge of the bonnet at right angles on to the curved edge of the bonnet back piece matching points A. Cut a 178 mm (7 in.) strip of very narrow ribbon and glue it to the bonnet as shown on the pattern, leaving equal lengths hanging down at either side of the bonnet to tie under the chin. Glue a small frill of gathered lace to the bonnet, close to the ribbon at the face edge. Glue a small frill of the same lace to the side and centre back edges of the bonnet to hang down over the neck. Make a few flowers by gathering up tiny strips of pink ribbon or fabric. Glue them on to one side of the bonnet. Glue the bonnet to the head setting it fairly far back. Glue a tiny ruffle of lace to the hair just inside the bonnet brim. Tie the ribbons in a bow under the chin.

Parasol Cut the parasol shape (piece 7, *figure 32*, page 59) from thin card, then mark on the lines radiating from the centre to the outer edges, using a ruler and a sharp pencil to inscribe these lines into the card. Bend the card gently along each of the inscribed lines. Bring the long straight edges together and hold them in position with a piece of sticky tape. Bring all the short straight edges together (as indicated by the arrows on the pattern), and hold them in position with bits of sticky tape. Spread the outside of the parasol thinly with glue and cover it with a piece of thin silky fabric, stretching and pulling the fabric until it fits the shape. Cut the edges of the fabric even with the edges of the parasol. Line the parasol in the same way. Glue braid, lace or other trimming to the outer edges of the parasol. For the handle, cut a 127 mm (5 in.) length of 2 mm (1/16 in.) diameter wooden dowelling, sandpaper it to a point at one end, then colour the wood black. Make a small hole through the centre of the parasol with a needle and push the pointed end of the handle through the hole to protrude about 13 mm (½ in.) on the other side, glue the handle in position. Tie a ribbon bow to the pointed end of the handle. Glue the parasol to the hand.

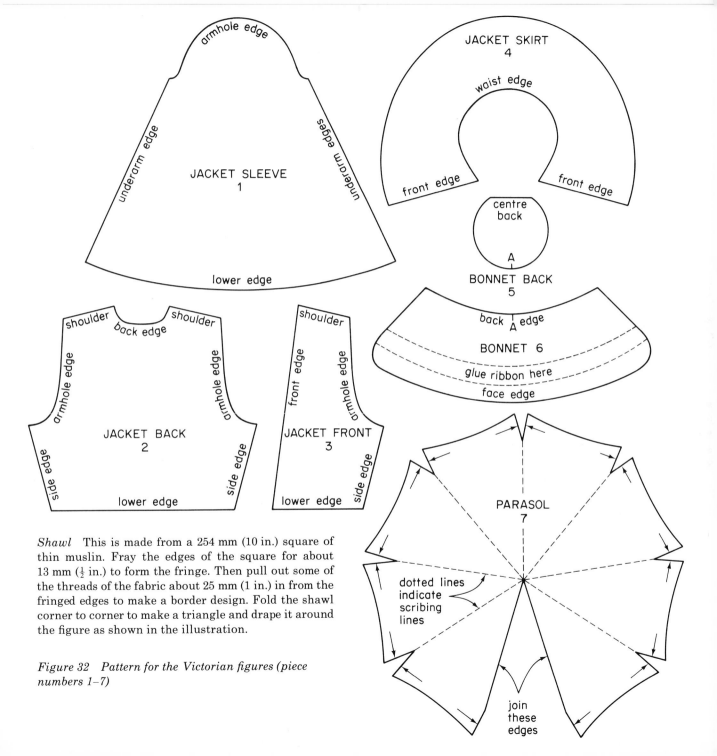

Shawl This is made from a 254 mm (10 in.) square of thin muslin. Fray the edges of the square for about 13 mm ($\frac{1}{2}$ in.) to form the fringe. Then pull out some of the threads of the fabric about 25 mm (1 in.) in from the fringed edges to make a border design. Fold the shawl corner to corner to make a triangle and drape it around the figure as shown in the illustration.

Figure 32   Pattern for the Victorian figures (piece numbers 1–7)

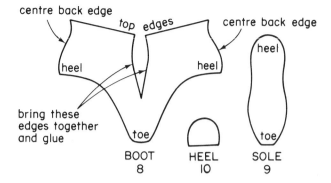

centre back edge · top edges · centre back edge

heel · heel · heel

bring these edges together and glue

toe · toe

BOOT 8 · HEEL 10 · SOLE 9

The father

He wears a peach-coloured silk waistcoat over a white shirt, with a green silk tie wound around the collar. His trousers are of checked woollen material and his black coat is edged with braid. On his head he wears a black silk top hat and he carries an ebony walking stick.

Make the basic figure, using chamois leather instead of felt for the hands to give the effect of gloves. Mark the backs of the gloves with three stitching lines as shown in the illustration.

Boots Cut two boots (piece 8, *figure 33*, page 60), two soles (piece 9, *figure 33*, page 60) and six heel pieces (piece 10, *figure 33*, page 60) from soft black leather. Glue the cut edges together, edge to edge, at the front of each boot as indicated on the pattern. Spread glue on the boot pieces and place them on the feet joining the centre back edges of the boots edge to edge at the backs of the legs. Push a little bit of wadding inside the boots at the heels to shape them. Glue the soles on to the boots pressing the edges of boots and soles together all round and at the same time pushing bits of wadding inside the boots to shape them. When the glue is dry, trim the glued edges with scissors to neaten. Glue the heel pieces on top of each other in two groups of three, then glue the heels in position under the boots. Bend the boot soles into shape to form the insteps.

Figure 33   Pattern for the Victorian figures (piece numbers 8–10)

Trousers Cut two trouser pieces (piece 11, *figure 34*, page 61) from check fabric taking care to reverse the pattern when cutting out the second piece to make a pair, as the lower edges of these trousers are shaped over the fronts of the feet. Turn the lower edges of the trouser pieces 3 mm ($\frac{1}{8}$ in.) to the wrong side of the fabric and glue them in place. Wrap one trouser piece around one leg of the figure having the lower curved front edge at the front of the figure, then overlap and glue the inside leg edges. Glue the other trouser piece on the other leg in the same way. Overlap and glue the centre edges of the trouser pieces at the centre front and back of the figure; the edges between the legs will not overlap, so glue these side by side. Glue the waist edges in position.

Shirt Cut a 50 mm (2 in.) square of white cotton fabric and glue it to the centre front of the figure just below the neck. For the collar, glue a piece of buckram on to a piece of white cotton fabric. Then cut out a 6 mm × 44 mm ($\frac{1}{4}$ in. × $1\frac{3}{4}$ in.) strip, glue this around the neck having the 6 mm ($\frac{1}{4}$ in.) edges meeting at the centre front. Cut a 3 mm × 50 mm ($\frac{1}{8}$ in. × 2 in.) strip of the stiffened cotton fabric and glue it down the centre front of the shirt piece. For the cuffs, glue 13 mm ($\frac{1}{2}$ in.) wide strips of the stiffened cotton fabric around the wrists. Glue two tiny white beads to the stiffened centre strip of the shirt for buttons.

Neck tie Wind a strip of very narrow ribbon around the base of the collar and tie it into a flat bow at the front.

Waistcoat Cut a 102 mm × 204 mm (4 in. × 8 in.) strip of silky fabric. Fold the strip in half widthways and iron the fold. Glue the two thicknesses of fabric together. Cut out two waistcoat fronts (piece 12, *figure 34*, page 61) placing the centre front edge of the pattern against the folded edge of the fabric. Turn the lower edges of the

Figure 34 (opposite)   Pattern for the Victorian figures (piece numbers 11–14)

waistcoat fronts 3 mm ($\frac{1}{8}$ in.) to the inside and glue in place. Fold back the fronts along the dotted lines for the lapels as shown on the pattern and glue them in place. Glue the waistcoat fronts to the figure at the shoulder, side and lower edges, then lap the left front edge slightly over the right front edge and glue in place. Glue four small beads down the left front edge for buttons.

Face, hair and beard   Using *figure 30b*, page 56, as a guide, colour the eyes, eyebrows and moustache brown. Colour the cheeks and mouth pink, marking other lines with pencil. For the hair and beard use dark brown wool which has been well teased out with a comb. Glue short strands of wool down the sides of the face and under the chin. Glue on strands of wool to cover the rest of the head.

Coat   This is made from thin black woollen fabric, but felt can be used as a substitute. Cut out two sleeves (piece 13, *figure 34*, page 61); then for the cuffs, turn the wrist edges of the sleeves 6 mm ($\frac{1}{4}$ in.) to the right side of the fabric and glue them in place, glue narrow black braid or cord to the sleeves to cover the raw edges of the cuffs. Place a sleeve on each arm, overlap and glue the underarm edges, then glue the armhole edges onto the shoulders. Cut out the coat back (piece 14, *figure 34*, page 61) and two coat fronts (piece 15, *figure 35*, page 63) taking care to reverse the pattern when cutting the second front piece to make a pair. Fold back the lapels on the coat fronts as indicated on the pattern and glue them in position. Overlap and glue the side edges of the coat fronts to the side edges of the coat back. Glue narrow black braid around the outer edges of the lapels, down the centre fronts and along the lower edges. Place the coat on the figure and glue the back piece in position at the shoulder and armhole edges, then glue the fronts in position at the shoulder and armhole edges. Glue the extended collar pieces on the coat fronts to the neck edge of the back of the coat for the back collar. Glue one small black bead to the right coat front at the waistline for a button.

Silk top hat   Cut two 102 mm (4 in.) squares of black satin fabric, then glue them to a 102 mm (4 in.) square of buckram, sandwiching it between the two pieces of satin. Cut out the hat side (piece 16, *figure 35*, page 63), the crown (piece 17, *figure 35*, page 63) and the brim (piece 18, *figure 35*, page 63). Overlap and glue the short edges of the hat side piece, then glue the top edge at right angles to the outer edge of the hat crown piece matching points A. Glue the lower edge of the side piece at right angles to the inside edge of the hat brim matching points A. Glue a strip of narrow braid or ribbon around the lower edge of the hat side for a hat band. Glue the hat to the head having points A at the centre back and front of the head. Turn up the brim at the sides of the hat.

Walking stick   Cut a 102 mm (4 in.) length of 2 mm ($\frac{1}{16}$ in.) diameter wooden dowelling and sandpaper it to taper to a point at one end. Colour the wood black, then glue a small gold or silver bead to the widest end for a knob. Glue the walking stick to the hand.

The child

She is dressed in the same fashion as her mother, her checked woollen skirt is worn over a crinoline and she wears a brown velvet jacket. Her long pantaloons are trimmed with lace and her elastic sided boots are made of cloth with leather toe-caps. She wears a large straw hat fastened under the chin with ribbons and she holds a wooden doll.

The basic figure for the child is made in a similar way to the larger basic figures. The wooden ball used for the head should be about 19 mm ($\frac{3}{4}$ in.) diameter. For the body and legs cut four pipe cleaners to 114 mm ($4\frac{1}{2}$ in.) in length and for the arms cut two pipe cleaners to 57 mm ($2\frac{1}{4}$ in.) in length. Glue all the pipe cleaners into the head, twist the body pipe cleaners together for about 38 mm ($1\frac{1}{2}$ in.). Turn up 13 mm ($\frac{1}{2}$ in.) at the end of

Figure 35 (opposite)   Pattern for the Victorian figures (piece numbers 15–21)

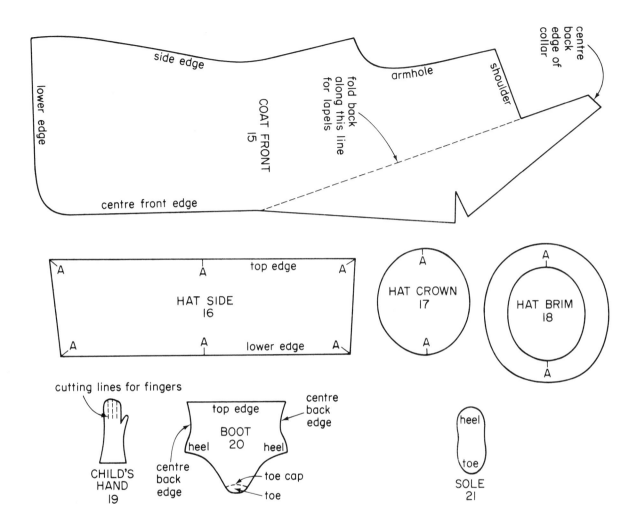

the legs, forming the feet. Pad the figure, keeping the amount of padding used in proportion.

Hands Cut four hand pieces (piece 19, *figure 35*, page 63) from thin cream-coloured or white leather to give the effect of gloves, taking care to reverse the pattern when cutting two of the pieces to make pairs. Glue to the ends of the arms in the same way as given for the adult basic figures. Mark the backs of the gloves with three stitching lines as shown in the illustration.

Boots Glue a 76 mm (3 in.) square of brown fabric on to another piece of thin material to prevent the fabric from fraying when the boot pieces are cut out. Cut two pieces (piece 20, *figure 35*, page 63) then glue on the toe-caps cut from thin leather as shown on the pattern. Spread glue on the boot pieces and place one on each foot, joining the centre back edges edge to edge at the back of the legs. Push a little wadding inside the boots at the heels to shape them, then cut out two soles (piece 21, *figure 35*, page 63) from thin leather and glue them in position, pressing the edges of the boots and soles together all round.

Pantaloons Cut two pantaloon pieces (piece 22, *figure 36*, page 65) from thin white cotton fabric then glue strips of narrow white lace trimming to the lower edges. Wrap one pantaloons piece around one leg of the figure and overlap and glue the inside leg edges; glue the other pantaloons piece on the other leg in the same way. Overlap and glue the centre edges at the centre front and back of the figure, then glue the waist edges in position.

Crinoline shape Cut a 44 mm × 178 mm (1¾ in. × 7 in.) strip of buckram. Using a needle and thread, run a gathering thread along one 178 mm (7 in.) edge. Then arrange the shape on the figure in the same way as given for the mother's crinoline.

Skirt A thin fabric with a small woven check pattern is used for this, but a plain fabric is also suitable. Cut a 64 mm × 229 mm (2½ in. × 9 in.) strip of fabric; turn one long edge 3 mm (⅛ in.) to the wrong side and glue in position for the hem edge. Glue a length of braid or other trimming to the skirt about 6 mm (¼ in.) above the hem edge. Using a needle and thread, run a gathering thread along the 229 mm (9 in.) raw edge, place around the waist of the figure. Pull up the gathers and fasten off. Overlap and glue the 64 mm (2½ in.) edges, then glue the folds of the skirt to the crinoline underneath to make it hang properly.

Undersleeves Gather up two short lengths of narrow white lace for each wrist and glue them in position.

Jacket This is made from brown velvet but thin wool is also suitable. Cut out two sleeves (piece 23, *figure 36*, page 65) and glue narrow braid or cord to the lower edges. Place a sleeve on each arm and overlap and glue the underarm edges. Glue the armhole edges onto the shoulders. Cut out the jacket back (piece 24, *figure 36*, page 65) and front (piece 25, *figure 36*, page 65), glue narrow braid to the lower edges and up the centre edges of the front. Glue the shoulder and armhole edges of the jacket back in position on the figure, then glue the shoulder and armhole edges of the jacket front in position. Overlap and glue the side edges of the jacket.

Face and hair Using *figure 30c*, page 56, as a guide, colour the eyes blue and the cheeks and mouth pink. Mark all other face lines with pencil. For the hair, use pale yellow wool, well brushed out. Cut 102 mm (4 in.) lengths of wool and glue the centre of these lengths to the centre top of the head. Glue the strands down each side of the face, then towards the back of the head. Leave the strands of wool hanging down the back of the figure and trim the ends even.

Hat The straw effect for the hat can be obtained by gluing pieces of cream-coloured curtain net on either side of a piece of buckram for stiffening. Cut out the hat brim (piece 26, *figure 36*, page 65) the hat side (piece 27, *figure 36*, page 65) and the crown (piece 28, *figure 36*, page 65). Glue the short edges of the hat side piece together overlapping slightly, then glue one edge of the hat side piece at right angles to the centre edge of the brim. Glue the edge of the crown at right angles to the edge of the hat side piece. Glue a narrow strip of ribbon around the hat side; tie it in a knot at the back of the hat leaving the ends hanging down. Glue the ends of two strips of narrow ribbon inside the hat brim at the positions indicated on the pattern. Glue the hat to the back of the head and tie the ribbons under the chin and in a bow at one side of the face. Turn down the brim of the hat above the face as illustrated.

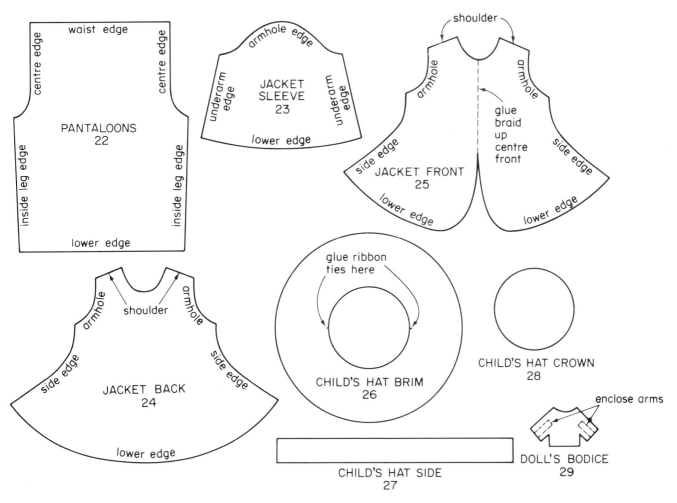

Doll For the doll's head use a small wooden bead measuring 6 mm to 10 mm ($\frac{1}{4}$ in. to $\frac{3}{8}$ in.) diameter. For the legs, pare down two match sticks to about 2 mm ($\frac{1}{16}$ in.) diameter and glue these together into the hole in the bead, colouring the feet black. For the arms pare down a match stick as for the legs, then cut off two 13 mm ($\frac{1}{2}$ in.) lengths. Cut two doll's bodice-pieces (piece 29, *figure 36*, page 65 from a scrap of fabric and glue

them to the front and back of the doll just beneath the head, enclosing the wooden arms between the pieces as shown on the pattern. Gather up a scrap of fabric and glue it in place for the skirt. Glue scraps of lace around the legs for pantaloons. Colour the hair black and mark on the face. Glue a scrap of lace to the head for a bonnet and glue on a length of thread to tie under the chin for ribbons.

Figure 36   Pattern for the Victorian figures (piece numbers 22–29)

A pirate—imaginative figure

The pirate has a peg leg, but on his good leg wears a striped stocking and a buckled shoe. His knee breeches are of black velvet. He wears an orange brocade waistcoat and a coat of pale green velvet edged with violet trimming. His black cocked hat is edged with gold braid and a parrot perches on his shoulder. He carries a spyglass.

Make the basic figure cutting one leg short just below the knee.

Note To give the pirate a rough appearance, the fabrics used should be faded or worn.

Pirate

Figure 37 Pattern for the pirate's face

Figure 38　A pirate

Stocking Cut the stocking (piece 1, *figure 39*, page 69) from striped fabric. Glue it around the leg, overlapping the centre back edges at the back of the leg. Glue the knee and ankle edges in position.

Shoe Cut the shoe (piece 2, *figure 39*, page 69) from thin black leather and the sole (piece 3, *figure 39*, page 69) and two heel pieces (piece 4, *figure 39*, page 69) from thicker leather. Spread glue on the shoe and place it on the foot covering the ankle edge of the stocking and joining the centre back edges, edge to edge at the back of the foot. Push a little bit of wadding inside the shoe at the heel to shape it. Glue the sole on to the shoe, pressing the edges of shoe and sole together all round and at the same time pushing bits of wadding inside to shape the shoe making it especially rounded at the toe. Glue the heel pieces on top of each other, then glue the heel in position under the sole. Bend the sole into shape to form the instep. Make a buckle shape from thick fuse wire and hammer it to flatten out. Glue the buckle to the front of the shoe as illustrated on top of a narrow strip of leather for a 'strap'.

Knee breeches Cut two knee breeches pieces (piece 5, *figure 39*, page 69) from black velvet. Wrap one breeches piece around the full length leg of the figure and overlap and glue the inside leg edges; glue the waist edge to the waist. Glue the lower edge in place to cover the top of the stocking, creasing the fabric as necessary to fit the leg. Glue the other breeches piece in position overlapping and gluing the inside leg edges, then gluing the waist edge in position. Gather up and glue the lower edge underneath the end of the shortened leg. Overlap and glue the centre edges of the breeches pieces at the centre front and back of the figure; the edges between the legs will not overlap, so glue these side by side. Tie a narrow strip of silky fabric around the full length leg at the lower edge of the breeches as illustrated.

Peg leg Cut a wooden ball or bead measuring 19 mm ($\frac{3}{4}$ in.) diameter in half and use one half only for the top of the peg leg. Cut a 57 mm ($2\frac{1}{4}$ in.) length of 6 mm ($\frac{1}{4}$ in.) diameter wooden dowelling and pare it down towards one end. Make a 6 mm ($\frac{1}{4}$ in.) diameter hole in the half wooden ball and glue the wide end of the dowelling into it. Glue the peg leg into position as illustrated. Trim the peg leg as necessary to bring it even with the other leg.

Waistcoat This is cut from the same pattern as the coat except that the lower edges are shortened slightly after cutting out. Cut the back (piece 7, *figure 40*, page 71) and two fronts (piece 8, *figure 40*, page 71) from brocade, taking care to reverse the pattern when cutting out the second front piece. Cut 6 mm ($\frac{1}{4}$ in.) off the lower edges of all three pieces. Glue lace, braid or other trimming to the centre front and lower edges of the front pieces and to the lower edge of the back piece. Glue the back piece in position on the figure at the shoulder and armhole edges, glue the front pieces in position at the shoulder and armhole edges lapping the shoulder edges of the back slightly. Overlap and glue the side edges of the waistcoat.

Belt Use a real metal buckle for the belt measuring about 13 mm × 19 mm ($\frac{1}{2}$ in. × $\frac{3}{4}$ in.). Cut a strip of leather wide enough to fit the buckle and long enough to go round the figure, plus a little extra for fastening. Thread the buckle onto the leather strip and fasten it at the front of the figure.

Wrist frills Glue a gathered up length of lace to each wrist so that it hangs down over each hand.

Coat This is made from a piece of old velvet. Cut out two sleeves (piece 6, *figure 39*, page 69), then cut each sleeve into two pieces along the cuff lines as indicated on the pattern. Turn the cuff pieces over and glue them back on to the sleeves in the same positions, overlapping the edges slightly. This is done so that the right side of the fabric will show when the cuffs are turned back over the sleeves. Glue braid or trimming to the right side of the lower edges of the cuffs, then for the

Figure 39 (opposite) Pattern for the pirate (piece numbers 1–6)

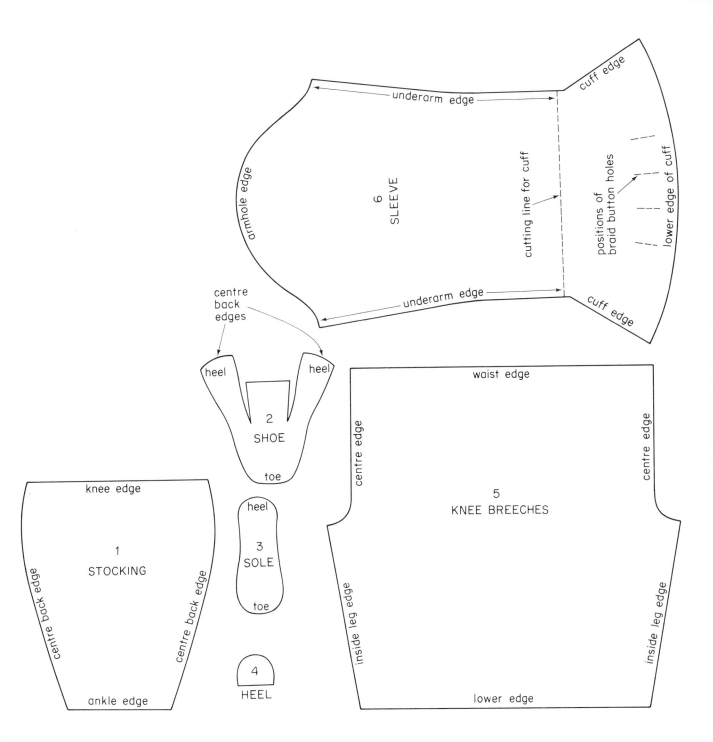

'buttonholes' glue on 3 mm ($\frac{1}{8}$ in.) wide cuttings of braid as shown on the pattern. Place a sleeve on each arm and overlap and glue the underarm edges down to where the cuffs are glued on. Turn back the cuffs and overlap and glue the cuff edges. Glue on beads for 'buttons' at the top edges of the buttonholes as illustrated. Glue the armhole edges of the sleeves to the shoulders. Cut out the coat back (piece 7, *figure 40*, page 71) and glue braid to the lower edge. Glue the coat back to the figure at the shoulder and armhole edges. Cut out two coat fronts (piece 8, *figure 40*, page 71) taking care to reverse the pattern when cutting the second piece to make a pair. For the pockets, glue two layers of velvet wrong sides together, then cut out two strips to the size indicated on the coat front pattern. Glue one pocket to each coat front then glue 'buttonholes' and 'buttons' on the pockets in the same way as for the sleeve cuffs. Glue braid to the centre front and lower edges of the coat fronts, then glue beads for 'buttons' all down the right front edge of the coat. Glue the shoulder edges of the coat fronts in position overlapping the back shoulder edges slightly. Glue the armhole edges in position. Overlap and glue the side edges of the coat.

Neck scarf Cut a 38 mm × 127 mm ($1\frac{1}{2}$ in. × 5 in.) strip of red silky fabric. Tie it around the neck in a single knot at the front, leaving the ends hanging down.

Face, hair and beard Using *figure 37*, page 66, as a guide, mark the eyes and eyebrows in black. Roll up a small triangle of flesh coloured felt and glue in place for the nose. Colour the cheeks pink. For the hair and beard use strands of brown wool teased out with a comb. Glue the strands all round the head, across the face and under the nose as illustrated.

Eye-patch Cut the eye-patch (piece 9, *figure 40*, page 71) from thin black leather and glue the top edge to a length of thin cord. Tie the cord around the head, having the patch over the left eye.

Cocked hat Use black felt for the hat. For the high crown, cut a 50 mm (2 in.) square of felt and wet it with a strong starch solution, then stretch and pull it over the top, dome-shaped end of a broom handle. Tie some thread around it to hold it in place until it dries. When dry, cut away the edges of the felt, leaving a smooth dome-shape about 13 mm ($\frac{1}{2}$ in.) deep for the crown of the hat. Cut the hat brim (piece 10, *figure 40*, page 71) from black felt, then glue the edge of the crown piece at right angles to the inside edge of the hat brim. Glue gold braid or trimmings to the edge of the brim then turn up the brim along the three lines indicated on the pattern using a little glue to hold the brim in position against the crown of the hat. Glue the hat to the head.

Spy glass This is made by gluing together three pieces of tubing of slightly differing diameters, cut from plastic ballpoint pen cartridges, caps or end pieces. Glue the pieces together, then paint the two smaller tubes gold, and colour the largest tube with black marker pen. Glue strips of gold braid around each end of the black section. Cut a small circle of clear plastic to fit the end of the black tube and glue it in position for the 'glass'.

Parrot Cut a 35 mm ($1\frac{1}{2}$ in.) length of pipe cleaner and bend it into a very shallow S-shape. Wind a little wadding around the shape making it fat at the centre for the body and tapering it towards each end for the head and tail. Wind sewing thread around the wadding to hold it in place. Cover the wadding with small coloured feathers gluing them on and smoothing them flat with a little glue. Use a few straight feathers for the tail, smoothing them with glue to taper to a point. Glue one contrasting coloured feather to each side of the body for each wing. Cut the beak pieces (piece 11, *figure 40*, page 71) from thin card and glue them to the pointed end of the head as illustrated. Colour the beak red and glue two tiny black beads in position for the eyes. Then glue the parrot to the pirate's shoulder.

Figure 40 (opposite)   Pattern for the pirate (piece numbers 7–11)

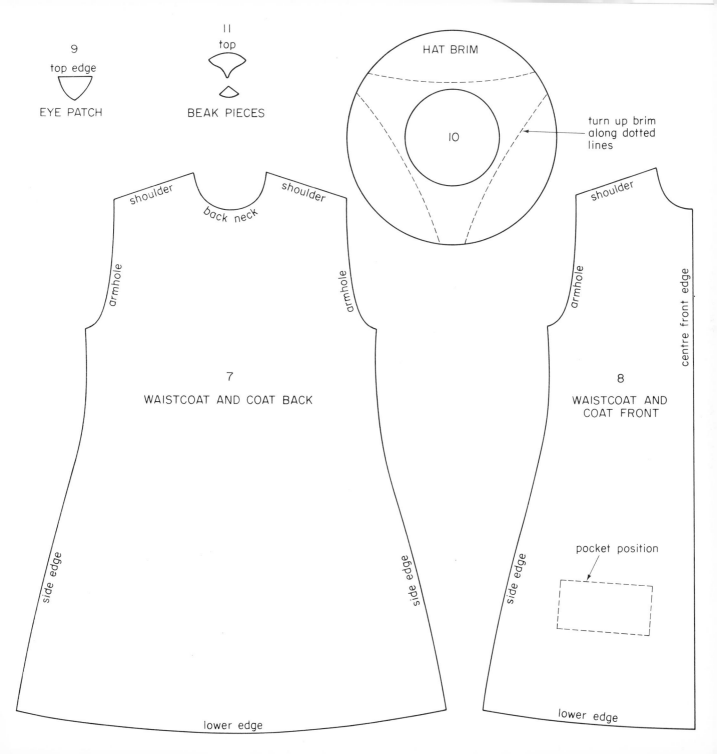

9
top edge

EYE PATCH

11
top

BEAK PIECES

HAT BRIM

10

turn up brim
along dotted
lines

shoulder

back neck

shoulder

armhole

armhole

7

WAISTCOAT AND COAT BACK

side edge

side edge

lower edge

shoulder

armhole

centre front edge

8

WAISTCOAT AND
COAT FRONT

side edge

pocket position

lower edge

Aladdin and the genie of the ring— fairy tale figures

Aladdin

At this point in the story he has been left in the cave by the wicked magician. In despair, he wrings his hands, accidentally rubbing the magic ring which the magician has given to him. Suddenly, the genie of the ring appears.

This figure is a little smaller than the basic figure. Make the arm pipe cleaners 102 mm (4 in.) long and add only 38 mm (1½ in.) extra length on to each leg. Glue on the hands, using the small hand pattern given for the woman's basic figure.

Face and hair   Using *figure 41a* as a guide, colour the eyes black and the cheeks and mouth pink. Mark all other face lines with a pencil. Using black embroidery thread for the hair, cut some 127 mm (5 in.) lengths and glue the ends to the head above and behind the ears. Take all the lengths to the back of the head and plait them together. Then tie a strand of thread around the end of the plait to keep the threads in place.

Undershirt   Cut a 38 mm (1½ in.) square of silky fabric and glue it to the chest of the figure just beneath the chin. Cut two sleeves (piece 1, *figure 43*, page 75) from the same silky fabric. Turn the wrist edges 3 mm (⅛ in.) to the wrong side of the fabric and glue in place. Place the sleeves on the arms of the figure, overlap and glue the underarm edges, then glue the armhole edges on to the shoulders.

A Aladdin

B Genie

Figure 41   Patterns for the faces of Aladdin and the genie

Figure 42   Aladdin and the genie

Shoes Cut two soles (piece 2, *figure 43*, page 75) from thin card, then glue these to another piece of card and cut around the first sole shapes. Continue doing this, building up layers of card until the soles are about 3 mm ($\frac{1}{8}$ in.) thick. Bend up the pointed toe ends of the soles. Glue each sole in position under each foot. Cut two shoe pieces (piece 3, *figure 43*, page 75) from black felt, spread the top edges of the soles with glue, then place a shoe piece around each foot. Press the edges of shoes and soles together all round and glue the centre back edges of the shoes together edge to edge at the backs of the feet.

Pants The legs of these pants are extra long to allow for the baggy folds around the ankles. Cut two pants pieces (piece 4, *figure 43*, page 75) from plain cotton fabric. Overlap and glue the inside leg edges of each pants piece then push one on to each leg, bending the shoes down in line with the legs in order to do this. Overlap and glue the centre edges of the pants pieces at the centre front and back of the figure, the edges between the legs will not overlap, glue these side by side. Glue the waist edges in position. Glue the lower edges of the pants pieces to the ankles and arrange the extra leg length in folds over the shoes.

Tunic This is made from a piece of brocade curtain fabric. Cut out the tunic (piece 5, *figure 43*, page 75) taking care to place the pattern piece against a fold in the fabric as indicated on the pattern. Glue narrow braid or trimming to the wrist edges then place the tunic on the figure and overlap and glue the underarm edges. Overlap and glue the side edges leaving the side splits open as indicated on the pattern. Glue narrow braid to the remaining raw edges as follows, beginning at the centre front neck edge, take the braid around the back of the neck and across the front chest to the side edge, take it down the side edge, then glue the braid to the raw edges of the side splits and the lower edges.

Hat Cut a 50 mm (2 in.) square of felt and make the crown of the hat in exactly the same way as for the crown of the pirate's hat on page 70. Glue a strip of narrow ribbon around the hat close to the edge. Glue a small circle cut from the same kind of ribbon, to the top of the hat for a flat 'button'. Glue the hat to the head.

Magic ring Glue a sparkling stone taken from a piece of junk jewelry on to one finger.

Magic lamp The lower part is made from one half of a cob nut shell. The flat top part is a piece of card cut to fit the half shell with one small hole cut in the centre and a smaller hole at the pointed end, then glued in place. The handle and base are strips of narrow braid or cord glued on. For decoration, glue on scraps of patterns cut off a gold doyley. Because the lamp is tarnished at this stage in the story, it should be painted a greeny-brown colour with the paint rubbed off here and there to show the decoration beneath.

The genie

He is a huge green figure, dressed in glittering garments and jewels.

The genie stands about 330 mm (13 in.) high and this larger-sized figure could be adapted to illustrate many other fairy stories which feature giants. Make the figure in the same general way as given for the basic figure but use a ping-pong ball for the head and pierce a small hole in it to glue the pipe cleaners into. Use two full length pipe cleaners for each arm and twist a full length pipe cleaner on to each of the four body pipe cleaners. Twist the four body pipe cleaners together for 114 mm ($4\frac{1}{2}$ in.), then twist the pairs of leg pipe cleaners together, turning up 25 mm (1 in.) at the ends for the feet. Pad out the figure, keeping the padding in proportion with the larger size. Make the legs very firm so that the figure will stand well.

Body, arms and hands These are covered with green fabric; this should be 'stretchy' and a piece cut off thick nylon socks, stockings or tights is most suitable.

Figure 43 (opposite) Pattern for Aladdin (piece numbers 1–5)

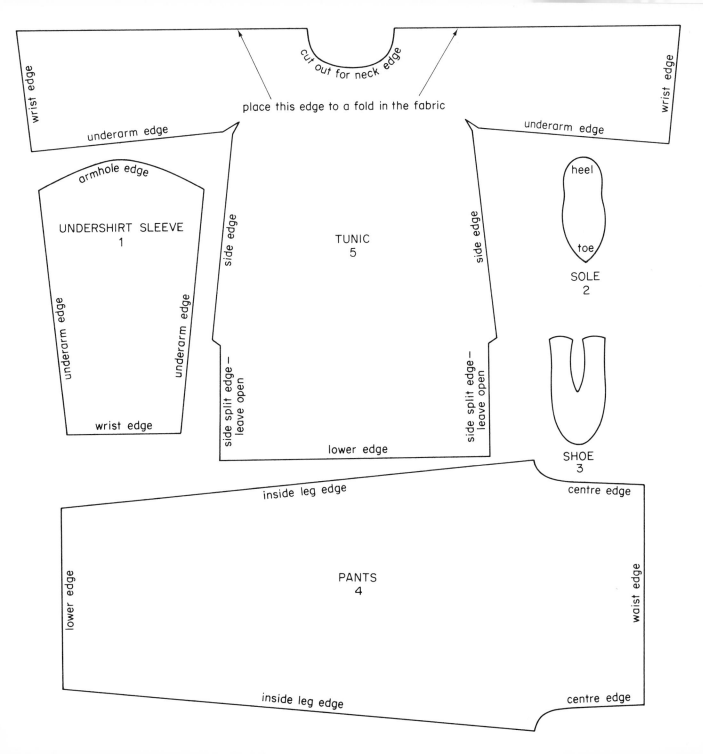

The fabric can first be boiled to remove the 'stocking' colour and then dyed green. A piece of green felt to match the green stocking fabric is used for the hands. Cut out four hand pieces (piece 6, *figure 44*, page 77) and glue them in pairs to the ends of the arms in the same way as given for the other figures. Cut out the body (piece 7, *figure 44*, page 77) taking care to place the pattern piece against a fold in the fabric before cutting out as indicated on the pattern. Push the head through the hole cut in the body piece, then glue the edge of the hole to the neck just beneath the head. Overlap and glue the side edges at the sides of the figure then glue the armhole and waist edges in position. Cut out two arms pieces (piece 8, *figure 44*, page 77), place one on each arm and overlap and glue the under-arm edges. Glue the wrist edges and shoulder edges in place. For a smoother finish, glue a second covering over the first. Glue strips of gold braid or trimming around the wrists for bracelets to cover the join.

Shoes Silver coloured leather is used, or ordinary leather, painted silver after the shoes have been glued into place. Cut out two shoes (piece 9, *figure 44*, page 77) and two soles (piece 10, *figure 44*, page 77). Spread glue on the shoe pieces and place one on each foot, joining the centre back edges together edge to edge at the back of each foot. Push a bit of wadding inside the shoes at the heels to shape them. Glue the soles on to the shoes pressing the edges of shoes and soles together all round and at the same time pushing bits of wadding inside the shoes to shape them. Turn up the pointed toes as the toe edges are being glued together.

Trousers These are made from two rectangles of lurex fabric. Cut out two pieces of the fabric 216 mm × 178 mm (8½ in. × 7 in.). Place one piece on one leg, having the 216 mm (8½ in.) edge along the length of the leg. Overlap the 216 mm (8½ in.) edges at the inside of the leg and glue from the ankle edge of the fabric to within about 76 mm (3 in.) of the top edge. Glue the other piece of fabric around the other leg in the same way. Overlap and glue the remaining 76 mm (3 in.) edges at the centre front

and back of the figure. Using a needle and thread, run a gathering thread around the ankle edge of each trouser piece, pull up the gathers and fasten off the threads, then glue the gathered edges to the ankles. Spread some glue on the waist edges of the trousers, gather into pleats and glue to the waist.

Waistband Cut a strip of striped fabric 64 mm × 457 mm (2½ in. × 18 in.). Wind this around the waist of the figure to cover the waist edge of the trousers. Knot the ends to hang down at one side and glue fringe or trimming to ends as illustrated.

Jacket Cut the jacket (piece 11, *figure 44*, page 77) from lurex fabric and glue gold braid or other trimming to the armhole edges and to the front and lower edges. Place the jacket on the figure and glue the front shoulder edges to the back shoulder edges, overlapping slightly.

Face and beard Colour the face green then, using *figure 41b*, page 72, as a guide, colour all the face lines black and paint the whites of the eyes white. For the beard, comb out some strands of black wool very thoroughly, then glue them beneath the nose and down each side of the face as shown in the figure.

Turban and fez The centre part of the head-dress, the fez, is made by covering a conical-shaped plastic lid with black velvet. Suitable lids can be found on containers for cosmetics and household cleaners. Glue the fez to the back of the head. For the turban, cut a strip of silky fabric about 50 mm (2 in.) wide by about a yard long and wind this around the head at the base of the fez as illustrated, gluing the end in place. A shorter length of fabric may be sufficient depending on how thick it is. Glue a sparkly button or jewel and feathers to the front of the turban.

Earrings Glue gold rings taken from an old chain to each side of the face at the base of the turban.

Pendant Hang a gold chain with a jewelled pendant around the neck.

Figure 44 (opposite)   Pattern for the genie (piece numbers 6–11)

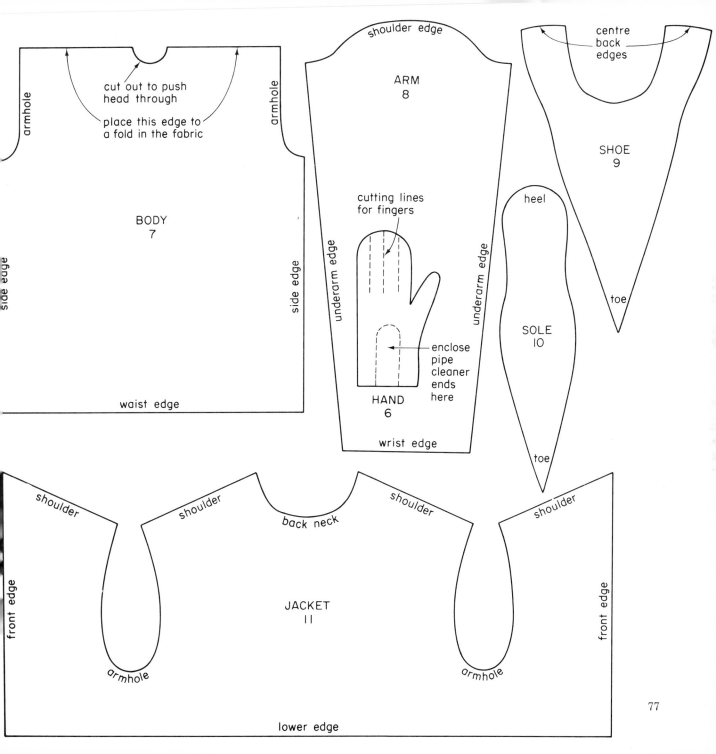

cut out to push
head through

place this edge to
a fold in the fabric

armhole

armhole

side edge

side edge

BODY
7

waist edge

shoulder edge

ARM
8

underarm edge

underarm edge

cutting lines
for fingers

enclose
pipe
cleaner
ends
here

HAND
6

wrist edge

centre
back
edges

SHOE
9

heel

toe

SOLE
10

toe

shoulder

shoulder

shoulder

back neck

shoulder

front edge

front edge

JACKET
11

armhole

armhole

lower edge

Circus figures—an auguste and a lady performer

The lady performer

She is a tall, elegant figure (she could be an acrobat, trapeze artiste or animal trainer). She enters the ring arrayed in a dazzling costume which glitters and sparkles in the spotlights.

Because this is a tall figure, make the pipe cleaners the same length as given for the man's basic figure. Pad out as given for the woman's basic figure, then cover with the nylon stocking fabric as instructed in the same section.

Face and hair Using *figure 45a* as a guide, colour the cheeks pink and the mouth red. Colour the eyes blue and outline them with black. Colour the area above the eyes pale blue, then mark all other face lines with pencil. Use pale yellow embroidery thread for the hair cut into 102 mm (4 in.) lengths. Glue the thread to the head winding it around to cover the head as illustrated, leave ends hanging down at one side of the face, spread them with glue and twist into a ringlet. Wind some lengths of thread around the top of the head for a 'bun' shape.

Tights A stretchy, knitted type of fabric is required for the tights and they are made from a piece cut off a sparkly nylon blouse. They can also be made from coloured nylon stockings or tights. The cloak lining is made from a piece of the same fabric. Cut out two tights pieces using the leg pattern given for the nylon covering on the basic figure, gluing them in position in the same way.

Léotard To make them fit properly, the léotard pieces should be cut on the 'cross' of the fabric. This is indicated on the patterns. Cut the léotard back piece (piece 1, *figure 47*, page 81) and the front (piece 2, *figure 47*, page 81) from lurex or shiny fabric. Glue the back piece to the back of the figure at the side, top and lower edges, pulling and stretching the fabric as necessary to get a good fit. Glue the front piece in position in the same way, lapping it over the back piece at the sides. For the shoulder straps, glue on strands of thread taken from cuttings of the fabric used for the léotard. Glue sparkly ric-rac braid over the leg and top edges, then glue narrow gift wrapping braid on top of the ric-rac braid. Make two small bows from braid and glue one to each side of the léotard at the tops of the legs.

A Lady performer

B Auguste

Figure 46 (opposite) Circus figures. An auguste and a lady performer

Figure 45 Patterns for the faces of the circus figures

Western saloon figures

High-heeled shoes   Cut four soles (piece 3, *figure 47*, page 81) from thin leather, then cut two 25 mm (1 in.) lengths of 15 amp fuse wire and glue the soles together in pairs, enclosing a length of wire between each pair. Bend each sole back at the line marked 'bend A' on the pattern, then bend them forward at the line marked 'bend B', to give the required arched shape. Glue a sole to each foot, bending the feet to match the shape. Cut two shoe toe pieces (piece 4, *figure 47*, page 81) from the same fabric as used for the léotard. Glue one to the toe of each foot, with the curved edges glued to the toe edges of the soles. For the high heels, cut two 13 mm ($\frac{1}{2}$ in.) lengths off a wooden lolly stick which measures about 3 mm ($\frac{1}{8}$ in.) diameter. Taper each heel by paring down towards one end, then sandpaper the other end to form a slight angle to fit against the heel ends of the shoe soles. Glue the heels in position. Glue the same narrow braid as used on the léotard all round the edges of the soles, then glue a small knot of braid to the shoe fronts for trimming.

Head-dress   Scraps of marabou trimming are used for this, but any soft fluffy feathers are suitable. Glue the feathers into the top of the 'bun', then glue a sparkly piece of jewelry such as an earring to the top of the head in front of the feathers.

Cloak   If possible, use a piece of the same fabric as used for the léotard for the cloak, and the same fabric as used for the tights for the lining. Cut a 229 mm × 305 mm (9 in. × 12 in.) strip of each fabric and glue them together round the edges. Glue silver ric-rac braid to three of the edges, leave one 305 mm (12 in.) edge plain. Using a needle and thread, run a gathering thread along the plain side. Pull up the gathers until the edge measures 76 mm (3 in.), then fasten off. Glue a length of thin cord to the gathered edge. Place this edge to the shoulders of the figure and tie the cord in front. Glue the gathered edges of the cloak in position on the shoulders.

The auguste

He shyly presents the lady performer with a plastic flower. He is comically dressed in enormous boots and baggy trousers. The tails of his coat curl up at the back and his cuffs are worn and frayed.

Make the basic figure wrapping extra padding around the waist and omitting the felt hands because this figure wears large gloves.

Socks   Cut two 50 mm (2 in.) squares of striped fabric and glue one around each leg having the lower edges at the ankles.

Boots   These are made from soft, worn leather. Cut out two boot pieces (piece 5, *figure 47*, page 81), two soles (piece 6, *figure 47*, page 81) and four heel pieces (piece 7, *figure 47*, page 81). Using a needle and thread, lace up the centre edges of each boot piece as shown on the pattern, drawing the centre edges together; tie the thread in a bow at the top of each boot piece. Place one boot piece on each foot and glue the centre back edges together edge to edge at the backs of the legs. Stuff the heel of each boot with wadding to shape it, then spread the soles with glue and position one under each boot piece, at the same time pushing bits of wadding inside the boots as necessary to shape them. Glue the heel pieces together in pairs, then glue one pair in position under each sole. Cut two 3 mm ($\frac{1}{8}$ in.) wide by 25 mm (1 in.) strips of leather and glue the 3 mm ($\frac{1}{8}$ in.) edges of each strip together to form a loop. Glue the loops to the top back edges of the boots for the 'pulling on' tabs.

Pants   Cut two pants pieces (piece 8, *figure 47*, page 81) from brightly coloured, checked or striped fabric; turn the lower edges 3 mm ($\frac{1}{8}$ in.) to the wrong side of the fabric and glue in position. Wrap one pants piece around one leg of the figure and overlap and glue the inside leg edges; glue the other pants piece around the other leg in the same way. Overlap and glue the centre edges of the pants pieces at the centre front and back

Figure 47 (opposite)   Pattern for the circus figures (piece numbers 1–8)

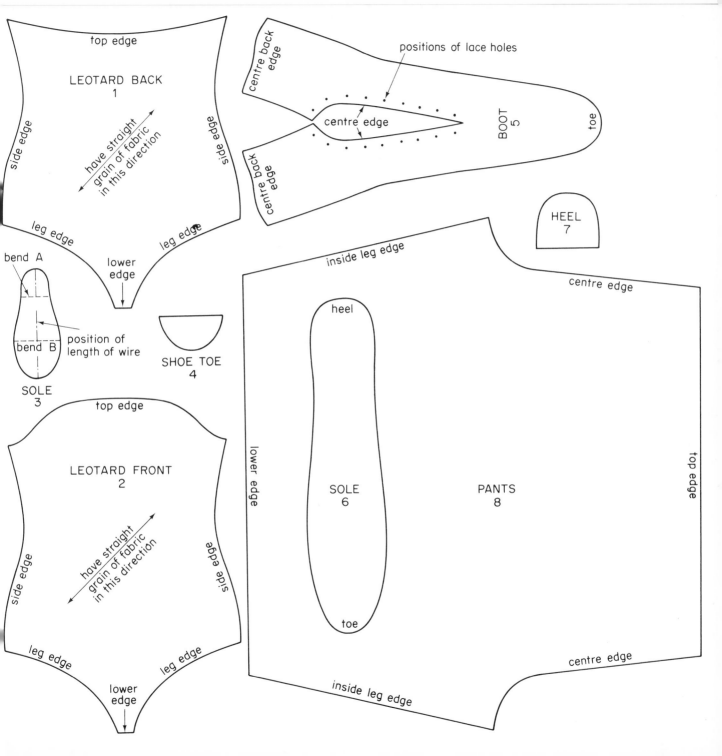

of the figure; the edges between the legs will not overlap, so glue these side by side. Glue the top edge of the pants as high up as possible creasing the fabric to fit the figure as necessary.

Gloves   Using white leather, cut out four glove pieces (piece 9, *figure 48*, page 83) taking care to reverse the pattern when cutting out the second part of each glove. To make the gloves flexible, wire is glued between each of the two pieces. Bend two lengths of 15 amp fuse wire into the shape shown on the glove pattern then glue these to two of the glove pieces. Glue the glove pieces in pairs to the ends of the arms enclosing the ends of the pipe cleaners as indicated on the pattern. Cut the gloves into fingers as shown on the pattern.

Dickey   The dickey, or false shirt front, is cut from a white plastic washing up liquid bottle. Use the inside (unprinted) surface. Cut out the dickey (piece 10, *figure 48*, page 83) having the curve of the bottle in the direction indicated on the pattern, fix five paper fasteners into the dickey at the positions shown on the pattern. Glue the neck edge of the dickey to the figure just beneath the chin.

Evening coat   This is made from thin black fabric but felt can also be used. Cut out two sleeves (piece 11, *figure 48*, page 83) and two coat pieces (piece 12, *figure 48*, page 83) taking care to reverse the pattern when cutting out the second piece to make the pair. Place a sleeve on each arm and overlap and glue the underarm edges. Glue the armhole edges on to the shoulders. The tails of the coat are wired so that they can be curled up and another layer of fabric is glued on to the wrong side of the tails to hold the wire in place. Cut out two tails lining pieces, using the cutting line indicated on the evening coat pattern as a guide. Glue the lining pieces in position on each coat piece enclosing a length of 15 amp fuse wire in each tail bent into shape as shown on the pattern. Fold back the centre front edges of each coat piece for the lapels as shown on the pattern and

glue in place. Position one coat piece on the figure and glue the armhole and shoulder edges in place lapping the front shoulder edge over the back shoulder edge. Glue the other coat piece in position in the same way. Overlap and glue the centre back edges of the coat pieces as far as the beginning of the tails.

Cuffs   Make these from white cotton fabric, tearing instead of cutting out, to get the frayed effect. For each cuff, tear off a 32 mm × 57 mm (1¼ in. × 2½ in.) strip of fabric. Fold each strip in half widthways and glue. Sew a button to each end of the cuff pieces, then glue the cuffs in place around the wrist edges of the sleeves.

Bald head, face and hair   Spread a little glue on top of the head, then use pink *Plasticine* to build up the bald head to give 13 mm (½ in.) extra height. Smooth the *Plasticine* into a dome-shape. For the hair cut 38 mm (1½ in.) lengths of orange wool, fold the lengths in half and glue the folded ends to the head all round at the lower edge of the *Plasticine*. Colour all the face to match the bald head then mark on the features using *figure 45b*, page 78, as a guide. Colour the mouth area deep pink and the areas above the eyes blue, then paint all other face lines black. Outline the mouth area with red, then with white. For the nose, glue on half a wooden bead painted shiny red.

Bow tie   Tie a length of ribbon around the neck in a large bow at the front.

Flowers   Glue a small plastic flower to the left hand. Make a flower 'buttonhole' from felt and glue it to the lapel.

Bowler hat   Cut a 50 mm (2 in.) square of black felt and make the crown of the hat exactly the same way as for the pirate's hat on page 70. Cut the hat brim (piece 13, *figure 48*, page 83) from black felt. Then glue the edge of the crown piece at right angles to the inside edge of the hat brim. Glue the hat to the right hand as illustrated.

Figure 48 (opposite)   Pattern for the circus figures (piece numbers 9–13)

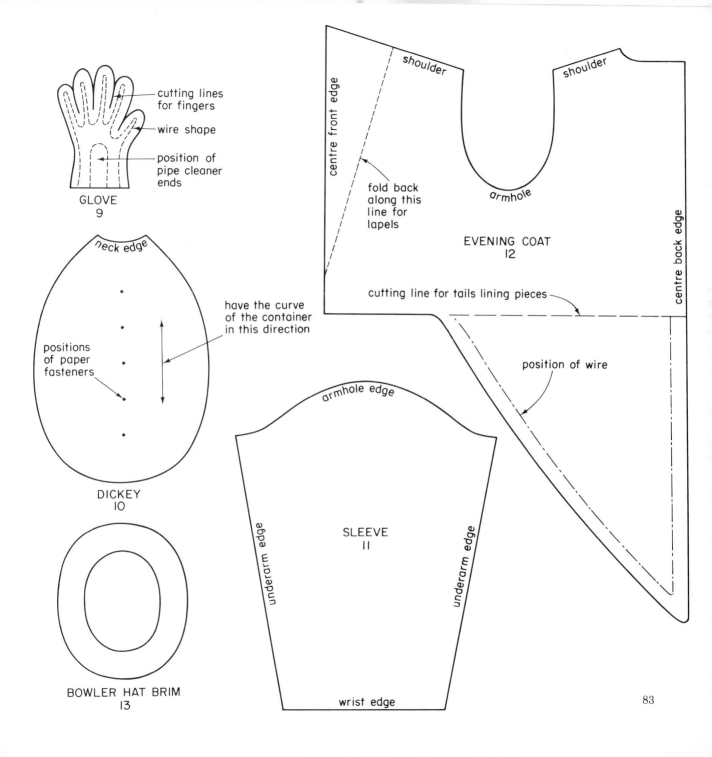

GLOVE
9

cutting lines for fingers

wire shape

position of pipe cleaner ends

neck edge

positions of paper fasteners

have the curve of the container in this direction

DICKEY
10

BOWLER HAT BRIM
13

centre front edge

shoulder

shoulder

fold back along this line for lapels

armhole

EVENING COAT
12

centre back edge

cutting line for tails lining pieces

position of wire

armhole edge

underarm edge

underarm edge

SLEEVE
11

wrist edge

Western saloon figures

The old timer

With his poke of gold, he tells everyone 'There's gold in them thar hills'.

This is a small figure and the basic figure must be made shorter. Make the arm pipe cleaners 100 mm (4 in.) long and add only 38 mm (1½ in.) extra length on to the leg pipe cleaners. Note that the lower edges of the shirt sleeves and the pants will have to be cut shorter to fit this figure.

Shirt Use cotton fabric with a small check pattern. Cut out the shirt (piece 1, *figure 56*, page 92) and two sleeves (piece 2, *figure 56*, page 92). Place the shirt on the figure, turn in the left front edge 3 mm (⅛ in.) and glue it in position, then glue it over the right front edge. Overlap and glue the side edges at the sides of the figure. On the right side of the fabric, spread glue across 6 mm (¼ in.) of the sleeve wrist edges, then turn up the edges 3 mm (⅛ in.) twice to form the sleeve cuffs. Place the sleeves on the arms and overlap and glue the underarm edges under the arms of the figure. Spread glue on the armhole edges of the sleeves and press them on to the armhole edges of the shirt. Glue a few small beads at intervals down the shirt for buttons. Cut the shirt collar (piece 3, *figure 56*, page 92) from two layers of the cotton fabric glued together. Fold the collar along the line indicated on the pattern and glue it around the neck.

Face Using *figure 49a* as a guide, mark the positions of the eyes on the head with pencil. From flesh coloured felt, cut the two small nose pieces using the outlines shown in the figure as patterns. Colour the eyes black and the cheeks pink, then glue on the nose pieces.

Hair and beard Cut a few 50 mm (2 in.) lengths of grey wool. Comb them to divide into finer strands. Glue the strands of wool to the head and across the lower part of the face for the beard then glue the centre of a strand of wool just under the nose for the moustache. Glue two short lengths of wool above the eyes for the eyebrows. Cut the ends of the hair and beard into shape as shown in the illustration.

Boots Cut two boot pieces (piece 4, *figure 56*, page 92) from soft leather. Cut two boot soles (piece 5, *figure 56*, page 92) and three of each of the boot heel pieces (piece 6, A, B and C, *figure 56*, page 92) from thicker leather. Spread glue on the boot pieces and place them on the feet joining the centre back edges of the boots edge to edge at the backs of the legs. Push a little bit of wadding inside the boots at the heels to shape them. Spread glue on the sole pieces and place the soles on to the boots. Press the edges of the boots and soles together all round and at the same time push bits of wadding inside the boots to shape them. When the glue is dry, trim the glued edges with scissors to neaten. Glue the two groups of heel pieces together on top of each other, then glue the heels in position on the soles. Bend the boot soles into shape to form the insteps.

A The old timer   B The stranger

Figure 49 Patterns for the faces of the old timer and the stranger

Figure 50 (opposite) The old timer and the stranger

Pants   Cut two pants pieces (piece 7, *figure 57*, page 93) and two pockets (piece 8, *figure 57*, page 93) from plain fabric; turn the lower edges of the pants pieces 3 mm (⅛ in.) to the wrong side of the fabric and glue them in place. Wrap one piece around one leg of the figure and overlap and glue the inside leg edges. Glue the other pants piece to the other leg in the same way. Overlap and glue the centre edges of the pants pieces at the centre front and back of the figure; the edges between the legs will not overlap, so glue these side by side. Glue the waist edge of the pants on to the shirt. Glue the pockets to the seat of the pants having a scrap of red fabric sticking out of the top of one pocket for a handkerchief.

Belt   Cut a 6 mm (¼ in.) wide strip of leather about 127 mm (5 in.) long. Glue it around the waist to cover the pants waist edge, overlap and glue the ends of the belt at the front of the figure and cut off any excess length. Make a buckle from fuse wire by bending it into an oblong shape, glue it to the belt at the front.

Vest   Cut the vest (piece 9, *figure 57*, page 93) from soft leather, then for the pocket flaps cut out two 3 mm × 15 mm (⅛ in. × ½ in.) strips. Having the suede side of the leather as the right side of the vest, glue the pocket flaps to the vest fronts near the lower edges. Make small marks with felt or ballpoint pen all round the edges of the vest for a 'stitched' effect. Place the vest on the figure and overlap and glue the shoulder edges.

Pipe   For the pipe bowl, cut a 6 mm (¼ in.) length off a round wooden lolly stick, make a little hollow in one end of the bowl and colour it black. Colour the outside of the bowl brown. For the pipe stem, pare down a match stick to make it very thin, then cut off a 25 mm (1 in.) length. Pierce a hole in the side of the pipe bowl and glue the stem into it. Pierce a hole in the head just under the moustache and glue the pipe stem into it.

Poke of gold   Cut a 50 mm (2 in.) by 13 mm (½ in.) strip of chamois leather, spread it with glue and fold it in half lengthways, enclosing a bit of wadding at the fold.

Tie lengths of sewing thread around the poke near the top, leaving loops of thread for draw strings. Glue the poke to the hand.

Hat   Cut the hat brim (piece 10, *figure 57*, page 93) and two high crown pieces (piece 11, *figure 57*, page 93) from dark grey felt. Join the two crown pieces together round the curved edges, taking care to spread the glue only along the very edges. Press and flatten the glued edges so that they butt edge to edge, making the crown a nice rounded dome shape with the join hardly visible. Glue the lower edge of the crown at right angles to the inside edge of the brim matching points A on each piece. Glue the hat to the head, having points A at either side of the head. Make a dent in the crown of the hat and turn up the brim at the front as shown in the illustration.

The stranger

He comes from the mountains, and has just ridden into town. He wears a buckskin shirt and pants and a coon skin cap.

Make the basic figure using leather for the hands instead of felt, to give the effect of gloves. Take care to cut the hands in pairs by reversing the pattern for two of the pieces when cutting out.

Boots   Make in exactly the same way as for the old timer on page 84.

Shirt   Glue a 38 mm (1½ in.) square of plain fabric to the front of the chest, just beneath the chin. This is the only part that will show after the buckskin shirt is glued on.

Buckskin pants and shirt   These are made from an old chamois leather. If the leather is very dirty it should first be washed in warm soapy water. Make the pants in the same way as for the old timer on page 86, omitting the back pockets. Cut the shirt (piece 1, *figure 56*, page 92) and two buckskin shirt sleeves (piece 12, *figure 57*, page 93) from chamois leather then cut the shirt front open from the neck as far as the point indicated on the pattern. Using a needle and brown sewing thread, lace the cut front edges together with a few cross stitches. Place the shirt on the figure and overlap and glue the side edges at the sides of the figure. Cut a 6 mm × 50 mm ($\frac{1}{4}$ in. × 2 in.) strip of chamois leather for the collar, glue it around the shirt neck having the front edges of the shirt folded back when doing this. Place the sleeves on the arms and overlap and glue the underarm edges under the arms of the figure. Glue the armhole edges of the sleeves on to the armhole edges of the shirt. Cut 13 mm ($\frac{1}{2}$ in.) wide strips of chamois leather and snip the strips across the width to make fringes. Glue the uncut edges of the strips of fringe to the lower edges of the shirt, along the sleeve underarms and over the shoulders at the tops of the sleeves. Cut two 15 mm ($\frac{5}{8}$ in.) squares of chamois leather for pockets, round off the lower corners and glue one to each side of the shirt front at chest height.

Neckerchief   Cut piece 13, *figure 58*, page 94 from thin red fabric. Place it around the neck and tie the ends at one side using a dab of glue to hold the knot in place.

Belt   Make in the same way as given for the old timer on page 86.

Face and hair   Using *figure 49b*, page 84, as a guide, colour the eyes black and the cheeks pink, then mark all other face lines with pencil. Cut short lengths of black wool and glue them all over the head and down either side of the face as shown in the figure. Leave a gap at either side of the head to indicate the positions of the ears.

Coon skin cap   A piece of real fur is used for this. If the pile is too long, trim it. Fur fabric can be used as a substitute. Cut a 20 mm ($\frac{3}{4}$ in.) wide strip, long enough to go around the head, then glue the strip in place, pressing the upper edges towards the crown of the head. Cut a small circle of fur for the centre of the cap to cover the crown of the head. Glue it in place. For the

racoon tail, cut a strip of the fur 13 mm × 50 mm ($\frac{1}{2}$ in. × 2 in.), tapering the strip slightly at each end. Using black felt pen, mark stripes across the strip then fold it in half widthways and glue the long edges together. Glue one end of the tail to the back of the cap.

The beautiful saloon owner

She wears a brocade dress, lace-up boots and feathers in her hair, (illustrated on page 101).

Make the basic figure.

Shoulders   Cut two shoulders (piece 14, *figure 58*, page 94) from flesh coloured felt. Glue one shoulder piece to the back of the figure having the neck edge touching the wooden ball. Glue the other shoulder piece to the front of the figure in the same way, lapping it over the back shoulder piece as necessary to fit.

Face   Using *figure 51* as a guide, colour the eyes blue, the cheeks pink, the mouth red and the eyebrows brown. Mark all other face lines with pencil.

Hair   Use tan-coloured embroidery thread. Spread the head with glue and taking a few strands at a time, wind the thread around the head to cover it completely. To make the ringlets use a thick bodkin or thin knitting needle, spread a little glue about 50 mm (2 in.) along the needle from the pointed end, then wind a strand of thread on to the glued portion working towards the point. Spread a little more glue over the wound round strands, then wind the thread over this, working back to the beginning. Pull the ringlet carefully off the

Figure 51   Pattern for the face of the saloon owner

needle. Make several ringlets of varying lengths and glue them in a bunch to the back of the head. Make two tiny ringlets on a darning needle and glue one to the hair at each side of the face. Take a large sparkly stone from an old brooch and a few feathers and glue them to the hair.

Stockings From a light coloured thin nylon stocking, cut two 25 mm × 76 mm (1 in. × 3 in.) strips. Glue one strip around each leg, having the 76 mm (3 in.) length along the leg and the joins at the back of the legs. Trim off any excess fabric at the join.

Laced boots Cut two boots (piece 15, *figure 58*, page 94) and two soles (piece 16, *figure 58*, page 94) from thin leather. Thread a needle with strong thread and sew the thread up the boot fronts for laces as shown on the pattern; pull the lacing tight and glue the thread ends in bows at the tops of the boots. Spread glue on the boot pieces and place them on the feet joining the centre back edges of the boots edge to edge at the backs of the legs. Push a little bit of wadding inside each boot at the heel to shape it. Spread glue on the sole pieces and place the soles on to the boots. Press the edges of boots and soles together all round and at the same time push little bits of wadding inside the boots to shape them. When the glue is dry, trim the glued edges with scissors to neaten. Make the boot heels by cutting two 6 mm ($\frac{1}{4}$ in.) lengths off a thin round wooden lolly stick. Sandpaper the heels at one end to taper them slightly, then glue the widest ends in position under the boots. Colour the wooden heels to match the boots. Bend the boot soles into shape to form the insteps.

Dress Use a sparkling fabric or satin. About 1·8 metres (1 yard) of gathered lace or trimming is also required. For the bodice, cut a 50 mm × 102 mm (2 in. × 4 in.) strip of fabric. Glue it around the figure under the arms to cover the lower edges of the felt shoulder pieces. Overlap and glue the 50 mm (2 in.) edges at the back of the figure, adjusting as necessary for a tight fit. Glue ric-rac braid or other trimming right around the lower edges

of the felt shoulder pieces. Spread glue along the arms and wind the gathered lace around to cover the arms to the wrists, this takes about 200 mm (8 in.) for each arm. For the skirt, cut a 89 mm × 416 mm ($3\frac{1}{2}$ in. × 16 in.) strip of fabric and glue gathered lace along one long edge. Overlap and glue the two short edges of the strip. Using a needle and thread, run a gathering thread along the untrimmed long edge, place the skirt around the waist of the figure, pull up the gathers and fasten off the thread. Tie a length of ribbon tightly around the waist to cover all the raw edges then glue the ribbon ends in a bow at the back of the figure.

Jewelry Glue a tiny, brilliant stone to one finger for a ring. Cut a very narrow strip of thin leather and glue it around the neck just beneath the head. Glue a sparkly stone underneath the leather strip for a pendant.

The young ranch hand

He sings and plays the guitar. He wears fancy angora chaps, high heeled boots and spurs.

Make the basic figure.

Face and hair Using *figure 52* as a guide, colour the eyes black, the eyebrows brown and the cheeks and mouth pink. Mark all other face lines with pencil. Glue short strands of brown wool all over the head and down either side of the face as shown in the figure. Leave a gap at each side of the head to indicate the positions of the ears.

Figure 53 (opposite) The young ranch hand

Figure 52 Pattern for the face of the young ranch hand

Shirt Make in the same way as for the old timer on page 84.

Neck tie Cut a narrow strip of red fabric, tie it around the neck and glue the knot at the front of the figure between the ends of the shirt collar.

Boots These are made from soft black leather in the same way given for the old timer except for the heels which are made from 9 mm ($\frac{3}{8}$ in.) diameter wooden dowelling. Cut two 6 mm ($\frac{1}{4}$ in.) lengths of dowelling (see *figure 54*, 1). Then cut a thin section off each one for the insteps (see *figure 54*, 2). Pare down the remaining curved edge to taper the heels (see *figure 54*, 3). Sandpaper the upper edges to slope down towards the instep (see *figure 54*, 4). Glue the widest part of the heels in position under the boots, then colour them to match. Bend the boot soles to conform with the shape of the instep.

Spurs These are made from fuse wire of different gauges, and two silver sequins. For one spur, cut a 38 mm ($1\frac{1}{2}$ in.) length of 30 amp wire, then trim off the edge of a sequin until it measures about 3 mm ($\frac{1}{8}$ in.) in diameter. Bend the wire into a wishbone shape and thread the sequin on to the wire (see *figure 55*). Squeeze the lengths of wire which lie on either side of the sequin together. Glue the spur around the back of the boot at the ankle, then bend the sequin end of the spur slightly downward. For the spur 'chains' which pass under the instep to hold it in place, cut two 50 mm (2 in.) lengths of 15 amp wire and twist them tightly together. Fold the length of twisted wire in half and glue it under the instep and up each side of the boot to meet the ends of the spur. Cut the spur strap (piece 17, *figure 58*, page 94) from leather and glue it across the front of the boot having the ends covering all the fuse wire ends at the sides of the boot. Screw up two tiny pellets of silver paper, press them flat, then glue one at each end of the spur strap for buttons. Make a small buckle for the spur strap from thin fuse wire and glue it in position at one side. Make the other spur in the same way, matching the position of the buckle on the other boot.

Pants Use denim fabric cut from old jeans. Make the pants in the same way as given for the old timer (page 86) but fold up the extra leg length to the outside for a deep turn-up before gluing the pants in position.

Belt Make as given for the old timer (page 86).

Vest Cut the vest (piece 9, *figure 57*, page 93) from soft leather, place it on the figure and overlap and glue the shoulder edges.

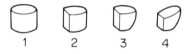

Shaping the boot heels

Figure 54 *Patterns for shaping the boot heels*

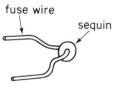

Shaping the spur

Figure 55 *Pattern for shaping the spurs*

Angora chaps An old sheepskin glove is most suitable for the front pieces of the chaps, using the fur outermost. The back pieces are made from soft leather. Cut two fronts (piece 18, *figure 58*, page 94) from the sheepskin, taking care to reverse the pattern when cutting the second piece of the pair. Cut two backs (piece 19, *figure 58*, page 94) from soft leather. Then cut two belt pieces (piece 20, *figure 58*, page 94) from thicker leather taking care to reverse the pattern when cutting the second piece of the pair. Glue the belt pieces to the upper edges of the front pieces in the positions shown on the pattern, then using a needle and strong thread, lace the front edges of the belt pieces together as shown on the belt pattern. Glue the sheepskin pieces about 3 mm ($\frac{1}{8}$ in.) over the leather back pieces at the outside leg edges. Place the chaps on the figure and glue the inside leg edges of the sheepskin pieces about 3 mm ($\frac{1}{8}$ in.) over the inside leg edges of the leather back pieces. Overlap and glue the belt at the back of the figure, over the left hip cutting off any excess length. Make a small buckle shape from fuse wire and glue it to the chaps belt at the overlap. Decorate the belt by gluing on small flat pellets made from scraps of silver paper.

Hat Cut the hat brim (piece 10, *figure 57*, page 93), the hat side piece (piece 21, *figure 58*, page 94) and the hat flat crown (piece 22, *figure 58*, page 94) from light grey felt. Glue the short edges of the hat side piece together overlapping slightly. Glue one edge of the hat side piece at right angles to the centre hole of the brim matching points A on both pieces. Glue the edge of the flat crown piece at right angles to the upper edge of the side piece matching points A. Cut a narrow strip of leather and glue it at the base of the hat side piece for the hat band. Glue the hat to the head having the join in the hat side piece at the back of the figure. Stiffen the hat by wetting it with a strong starch solution, curl the brim and dent the crown as illustrated, then leave to dry.

Guitar Glue some brown wrapping paper on to a piece of thin card. When the glue is dry, cut two guitar body pieces (piece 23, *figure 59*, page 95). Then cut out the centre hole on one of the pieces only. Cut out the guitar arm (piece 24, *figure 59*, page 95) and a 9 mm ($\frac{3}{8}$ in.) wide by 190 mm ($7\frac{1}{2}$ in.) long strip for the sides of the guitar. Spread glue along one edge of the strip and, beginning at the centre top, press it at right angles on to the edge of one guitar body piece keeping the edges as even as possible. Cut off any excess length when the short edges of the strip meet. Glue the other guitar body piece in position on to the other edge of the strip. Make marks around the centre hole and near the outer edges of the guitar body pieces as shown in the illustration. On the guitar arm, fold back the side pieces along the dotted lines indicated on the pattern and glue the shaped back edges together. Fold the top rectangular pieces to the back of the arm and glue them on top of each other. Make marks across the arm to indicate the 'frets'. Glue the arm to the guitar as shown on the guitar body pattern having the guitar arm edges marked A glued to the side piece of the guitar. For the strings, cut six 152 mm (6 in.) lengths of strong sewing thread; for the bridge cut a small strip of thick leather to the size shown on the guitar body pattern. Glue the ends of the strings to the bridge, spacing them out evenly. Leave until the glue is dry then glue the bridge to the guitar. Spread glue on the end of the guitar arm and position the strings evenly in the glue keeping them as taut as possible. Cut the excess length off the ends of the strings then glue three small beads to each side of the end of the arm piece for tuning knobs. When the glue is dry, bend back the top part of the arm slightly until it touches the edges marked B on the pattern, glue it in this position. Paint the guitar with clear nail varnish.

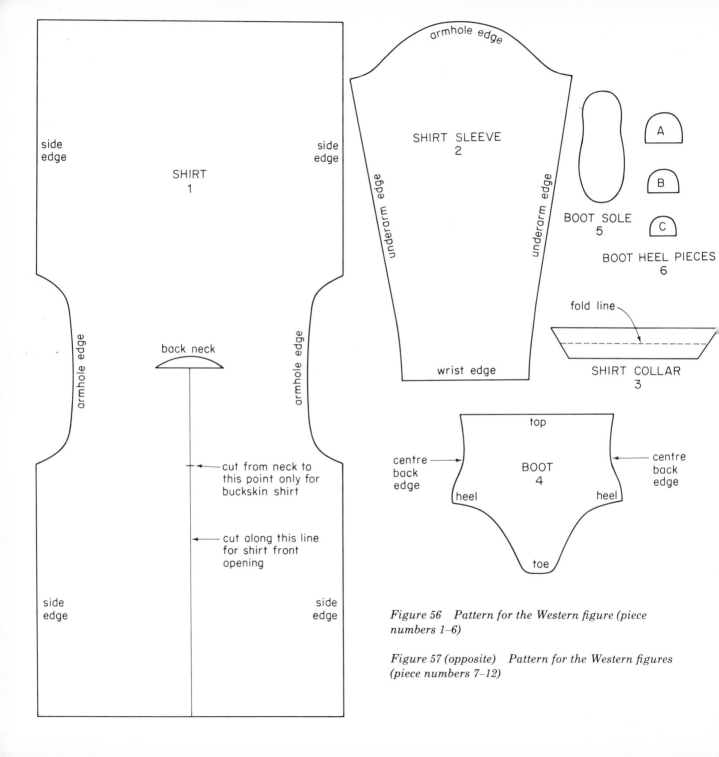

Figure 56   Pattern for the Western figure (piece numbers 1–6)

Figure 57 (opposite)   Pattern for the Western figures (piece numbers 7–12)

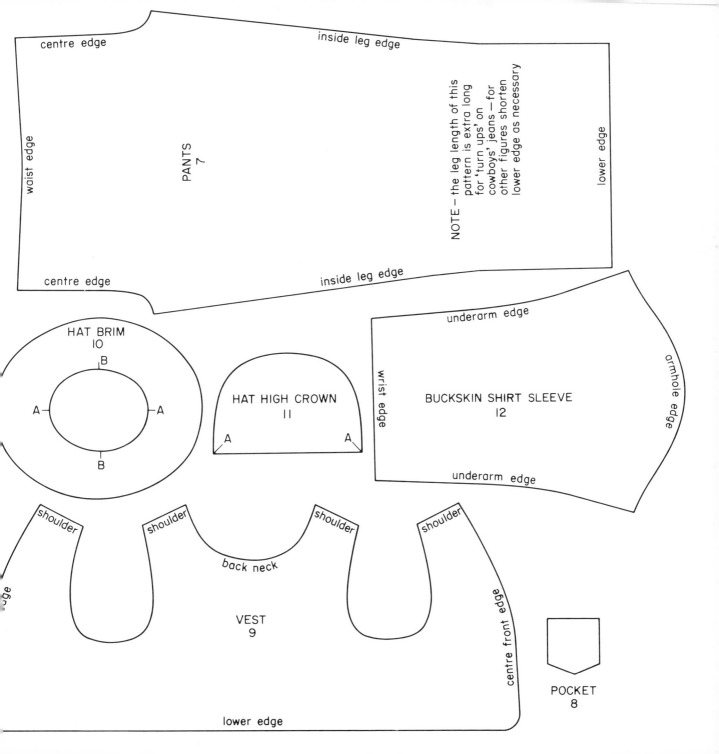

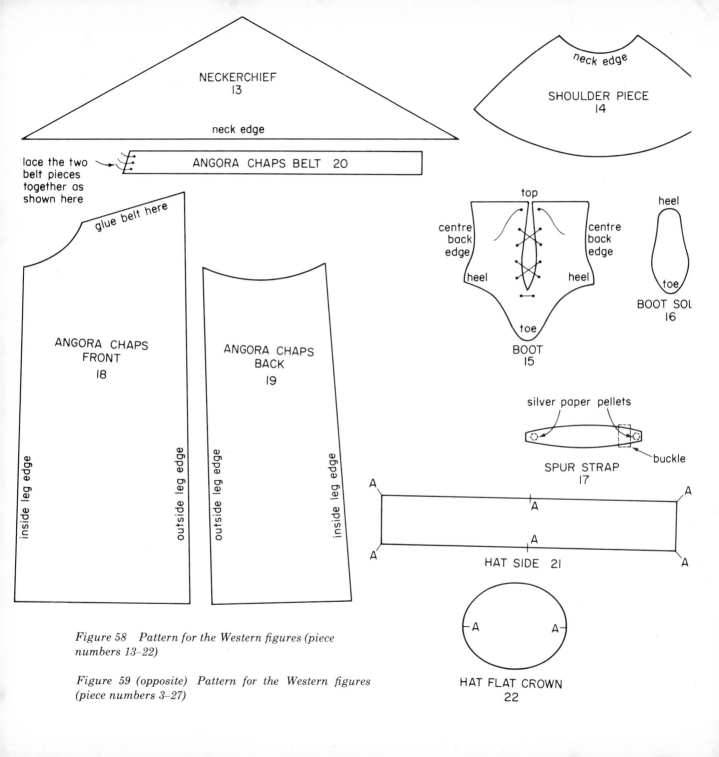

NECKERCHIEF
13

neck edge

neck edge

SHOULDER PIECE
14

lace the two belt pieces together as shown here

ANGORA CHAPS BELT 20

glue belt here

ANGORA CHAPS
FRONT
18

inside leg edge

outside leg edge

ANGORA CHAPS
BACK
19

outside leg edge

inside leg edge

top

centre back edge

centre back edge

heel

heel

toe

BOOT
15

heel

toe

BOOT SOL
16

silver paper pellets

SPUR STRAP
17

buckle

A   A   A

A   A   A

HAT SIDE 21

A   A

HAT FLAT CROWN
22

Figure 58   Pattern for the Western figures (piece numbers 13–22)

Figure 59 (opposite)   Pattern for the Western figures (piece numbers 3–27)

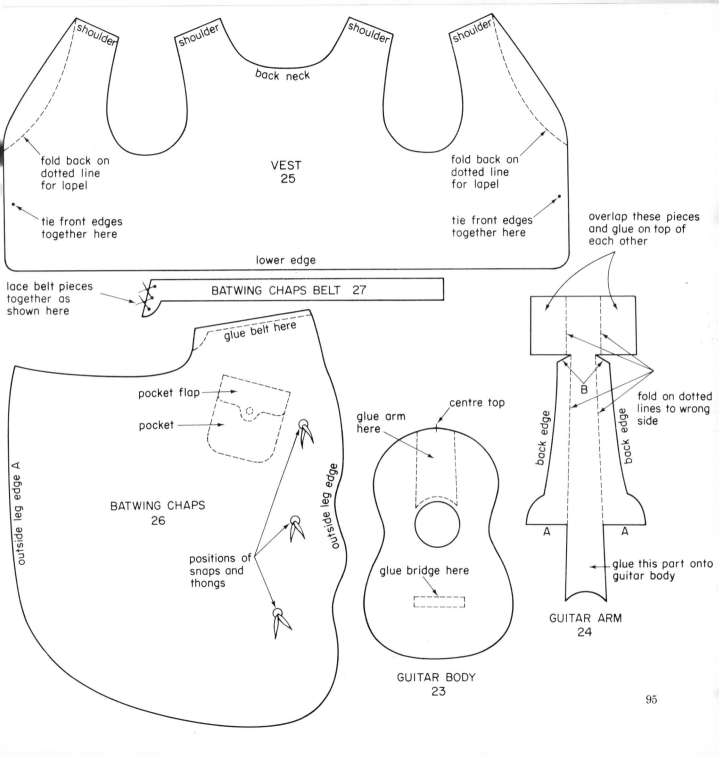

shoulder shoulder shoulder shoulder

back neck

VEST
25

fold back on
dotted line
for lapel

fold back on
dotted line
for lapel

tie front edges
together here

tie front edges
together here

overlap these pieces
and glue on top of
each other

lower edge

lace belt pieces
together as
shown here

BATWING CHAPS BELT 27

glue belt here

pocket flap

pocket

B

fold on dotted
lines to wrong
side

back edge

back edge

outside leg edge A

outside leg edge

centre top

glue arm
here

BATWING CHAPS
26

positions of
snaps and
thongs

A

A

glue this part onto
guitar body

glue bridge here

GUITAR ARM
24

GUITAR BODY
23

95

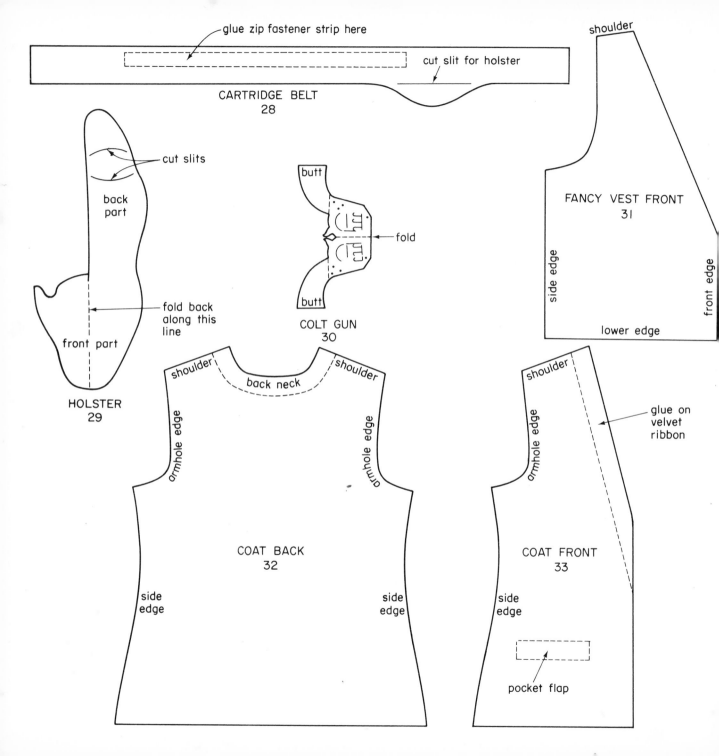

glue zip fastener strip here

cut slit for holster

CARTRIDGE BELT
28

shoulder

cut slits

back
part

FANCY VEST FRONT
31

side edge

front edge

fold back
along this
line

front part

HOLSTER
29

butt

fold

butt

COLT GUN
30

lower edge

shoulder

back neck

shoulder

armhole edge

armhole edge

COAT BACK
32

side
edge

side
edge

shoulder

glue on
velvet
ribbon

armhole edge

COAT FRONT
33

side
edge

pocket flap

The ranch foreman

He is dressed in full cowboy 'war paint'. He wears brown steerhide batwing chaps; also high-heeled boots, spurs, cartridge belt, holster and a colt gun.

Make the basic figure.

Face and hair Using *figure 61* as a guide, colour the eyes blue, the eyebrows brown and the cheeks and mouth pink. Mark all other face lines with pencil. Glue short lengths of brown embroidery thread all over the head and down either side of the face. Leave a gap at each side of the face to indicate the positions of the ears.

Neckerchief Cut the neckerchief (piece 13, *figure 58*, page 94) from thin red fabric, place it around the neck and tie the ends at the back of the figure using a dab of glue to hold the knot in place.

Shirt, boots, spurs, pants and belt Make in exactly the same way as given for the young ranch hand on page 90.

Vest Cut the vest (piece 25, *figure 59*, page 95) from soft leather, then fold back the front edges along the dotted lines indicated on the pattern for the lapels, glue in position. Place the vest on the figure and overlap and glue the shoulder edges. Cut a very thin strip of leather, thread it through the vest front edges at the positions indicated on the pattern. Tie the ends together.

Batwing chaps Cut two pieces (piece 26, *figure 59*, page 95) from soft, worn leather taking care to reverse the pattern when cutting out the second piece to make a pair. From the same sort of leather cut out two pockets and two pocket flaps as indicated by the dotted lines on the pattern; glue them in position on the chaps. Cut two belt pieces (piece 27, *figure 59*, page 95) from leather taking care to reverse the pattern when cutting out the second piece to make a pair. Glue the belt pieces to the upper edges of the chaps pieces as shown on the pattern, then using a needle and thread, lace the front belt edges together as shown on the belt pattern. Make small pellets from scraps of silver paper, flatten them and glue one to each pocket flap and three down each outside leg edge as shown on the pattern. Cut very thin strips of leather about 25 mm (1 in.) in length for the thongs and glue one folded in half to the centre of each snap as shown on the pattern. Place the chaps on the figure taking the outside leg edges marked A between and around the backs of the legs; glue these edges to the wrong side of the chaps in line with the top two snaps and thongs. Overlap and glue the chaps belt at the back of the figure over the left hip cutting off any excess length. Make a small buckle from fuse wire and glue it to the chaps belt at the overlap.

The ranch foreman

Figure 60 (opposite)   Pattern for the Western figures (piece numbers 28–33)

Figure 61   Pattern for the face of the ranch foreman

Cartridge belt   This belt is for a right-hand gun, the pattern must be reversed for a left-hand gun. Cut the belt (piece 28, *figure 60*, page 96) from leather, then cut a slit for the holster as shown on the pattern. For the cartridges, cut a 76 mm (3 in.) strip of metal teeth from one side of a metal zip fastener. Cut away as much of the fabric as possible. Glue the strip to the belt as shown on the pattern. Cut a 3 mm × 25 mm (⅛ in. × 1 in.) strip of the same leather as used for the cartridge belt for the front fastening. Place the belt on the figure, overlap the front edges about 6 mm (¼ in.) and glue. Glue the front fastening strip over this join, then make a buckle from fuse wire, hammer it flat and glue it to the centre of the strip. The belt should hang loosely over the hips.

Holster   This holster is for a right-hand gun – the pattern must be reversed for a left-hand gun. Cut the holster (piece 29, *figure 60*, page 96) from the same sort of leather as the cartridge belt. Cut the two slits in the back part as shown on the pattern, then fold back the front part along the dotted line indicated and glue the outside edges of the leather together where they meet. Push the back part of the holster through the slit in the cartridge belt, then push the front part of the holster through the slits in the back part so that the area between the slits forms a strap which keeps the holster in place.

Colt gun   Cut the gun (piece 30, *figure 60*, page 96) from thin card. For the gun barrel cut a 25 mm (1 in.) length from an empty ballpoint pen cartridge and cut a 19 mm (¾ in.) length of 30 amp fuse wire. Spread the gun with glue and fold it in half around the end of the barrel and the fuse wire. Cut a 13 mm (½ in.) length of 30 amp wire for the trigger guard and a scrap of 15 amp wire for the trigger. Shape and glue them into the gun as shown in *figure 62*. Press the two thicknesses of card firmly together so that all the extra pieces are glued firmly between them. For the gun butt use pieces cut from the compressed paper type of egg box which has a criss-cross surface texture. Cut two butt pieces using the gun pattern as a guide, then glue one on either side

of the gun and colour them brown. Colour the rest of the gun black with a permanent marker pen, then mark on the cylinder details as shown on the pattern using a white pencil or paint. Paint the gun butt with clear nail varish to make it shine.

Hat   Cut the hat brim (piece 10, *figure 57*, page 93) and two high crown pieces (piece 11, *figure 57*, page 93) from light grey felt. Make the hat in the same way as given for the old timer (see page 86) but glue the crown to the brim matching points A on the crown to points B on the brim. Plait three very narrow strips of leather for the hat band and glue it around the base of the crown. Glue the hat to the head having the joins in the crown pieces at either side of the head. Stiffen the hat by wetting it with a strong starch solution, curl up the brim and dent the crown as illustrated, then leave to dry.

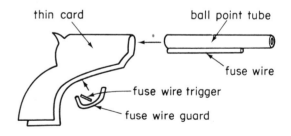

Assembling the colt gun pieces

Figure 63 (opposite)   The ranch foreman. The back view figure is the 'baddie'

Figure 62   Pattern for the colt gun

The gambler

He wears a frilled shirt, fancy vest, striped pants and a black coat with a velvet collar.

Make the basic figure.

Face and hair Using *figure 64* as a guide, colour the eyes black, the eyebrows brown and the cheeks and mouth pink. Mark all other face lines with pencil. Glue short lengths of tan embroidery thread all over the head and down either side of the face as shown in the figure, leaving a gap at each side of the head to indicate the positions of the ears.

Boots Make in exactly the same way as for the old timer (see page 84).

Shirt Cut a 50 mm (2 in.) square of white cotton fabric and glue it to the front of the chest just beneath the chin. Glue the edges of strips of very narrow white lace down the centre front of the shirt piece for a ruffle. Glue double strips of the same narrow lace to the wrists for cuff ruffles, then glue narrow strips of white cotton fabric behind the ruffles for the shirt cuffs. Cut the shirt collar (piece 3, *figure 56*, page 92) from two layers of white cotton fabric glued together. Fold the collar along the line indicated on the pattern and glue it around the neck so that the edges meet at the front of the figure.

Neck tie Using narrow black ribbon, make a bow and glue it to the shirt neck.

Pants These are made from black fabric with a narrow white stripe in the same way as given for the old timer (page 86), but omitting the back pockets.

Fancy vest front Cut two vest front pieces (piece 31, *figure 60*, page 96) from a brightly coloured shiny fabric taking care to reverse the pattern when cutting the second piece to make a pair. Turn the front and lower edges 3 mm ($\frac{1}{8}$ in.) to the wrong side of the fabric and glue them in place. Glue the vest fronts to the front of the figure, lapping the left front edge over the right

Figure 65 (opposite)   The gambler and the saloon owner

front edge. Glue four small sparkly stones at intervals down the left front edge for buttons.

Coat Use thin black woollen fabric or felt for the coat. A short length of 6 mm ($\frac{1}{4}$ in.) wide velvet ribbon is also required for the collar and pocket flaps. Cut out the coat back (piece 32, *figure 60*, page 96) and two fronts (piece 33, *figure 60*, page 96) taking care to reverse the coat front pattern when cutting the second piece to make the pair. Using the buckskin shirt sleeve pattern (piece 12, *figure 57*, page 93) cut out two sleeves. Glue the coat front to the coat back at the shoulders. Place the coat on the figure and overlap and glue the side edges at the sides of the figure. Place the sleeves on the arms and overlap and glue the underarm edges under the arms of the figure. Glue the armhole edges of the sleeves on to the armhole edges of the coat. Glue a strip of velvet ribbon to the neck and front edges of the coat for the lapels and collar as shown on the pattern. Glue short lengths of velvet ribbon to the coat fronts for the pocket flaps. Glue three small black beads near the right front edge of the coat for buttons.

Hat Using black felt, make the hat in the same way as given for the young ranch hand on page 91. Make the hat side piece (piece 21, *figure 58*, page 94) a little wider to make the crown of the hat higher.

The gambler

Figure 64   Pattern for the face of the gambler

Some other saloon characters – the piano player

He wears ordinary pants and boots and a double-breasted velvet vest. His striped shirt has arm bands. He wears a black bowler hat made in the same way as the auguste on page 82. He smokes a cigar made from brown paper.

The singer

Made in a similar way to the beautiful saloon owner. Cover the arms by winding round narrow strips of black lace for gloves.

The Mexican ranch owner

He wears grey pants flared at the hems and trimmed with silvery braid down the sides. His white shirt has a cravat at the neck and a broad red sash is tied around his waist. His black jacket is cut from a vest pattern slightly enlarged; the silver ornaments are made from fuse wire and glued to the front. To make the sombrero, wet a piece of grey felt with starch solution and stretch and tie it over a lid which measures about 57 mm (2¼ in.) in diameter. Leave to dry, then trim the edges. Leave the sequins full size for his spurs and clip them into points all round.

The sheriff

He wears woollen pants with boots glued over them, extend the top of the boots pattern for this. His shirt has loose cuffs turned back and the hand pattern is extended slightly up the arm. He wears a 'string' bow tie and his vest front is chamois leather, the back is cloth. The star glued to the left side of his shirt is cut from thick metal foil. His cartridge belt, holster and gun are made in the usual way.

The baddie

He is dressed completely in black. He wears high heeled boots, spurs, pants, shirt, neckerchief and vest. His hat has a flat brim and flat topped crown. He wears two guns and the cartridge belt should be adapted so as to have two slits for a left and right hand gun. The guns are painted silver and have black butts decorated with fuse wire. The lower tips of the holsters are tied to his legs using thick thread. He is obviously a 'fast gun'.

The Doc

A fat figure, so all pattern pieces are enlarged to fit him. He wears grey pants, a blue shirt and a maroon vest with a gold watch chain cut from junk jewellery. His jacket is dark grey and his boots are brown. His hair is grey and he smokes a cigar made from brown paper. The top hat is made like a cowboy hat but with a narrower brim and a high flat crown.

The bartender

He is the only man in the saloon without a hat. He wears wool'pants, a white shirt with arm bands and a thin 'bootlace' tie. His vest has a fancy front and the white apron is tied around his waist and reaches almost to his feet.

Other cowboys

They are all dressed in a style similar to those already given.

Materials used for the saloon – the walls

Use stiff corrugated cardboard cut from grocery boxes. The lower half is marked and painted to resemble wooden planks. The upper half is covered with fabric.

The base

Use a piece of insulation board, painted and marked to resemble wooden planks.

Oil lamps

Each one is made from a ping-pong ball, a metal hook, braid, a bead, and a rosette cut from a gold paper doyley for the wall bracket. The centre chimney is a length of clear plastic tubing.

The window

This is a piece of glass, the letters are cut from newspaper headlines after being inked in to make them a little more elaborate. The lower half is covered with tracing paper marked into a pattern of diamonds. The window frame and struts are strips of balsa wood.

The tables

These are round cheese boxes glued on to toilet roll tubes and painted brown.

The chairs

Seats and backrests are cut from a sheet of compressed cork; then round wooden lolly sticks and dowelling are pushed into the cork seats and backrests for the legs and back struts and glued in place. They are painted brown.

The piano

This is also cut from sheet cork. The carved panels are rectangles of black lace and strips of braid glued on. The front pillars are wooden balls glued on top of plastic *Drima* sewing thread reels. The keys are copied from a real piano and drawn on a strip of white card. The piano is painted brown.

The stool

This is made from a plastic lid glued on to a *Drima* reel. Braid is glued on for a carved effect and a small lid and three beads make a base. It is painted brown.

The gilt mirror

A small mirror is glued on to a piece of card larger than itself. A variety of braids are then glued to the card around the mirror and the braid painted with gold paint.

The shelves

These are strips of balsa wood glued on to cardboard backs. Cut pieces out of the walls behind the bar so that the shelves may be slotted in.

The drinking glasses

Make these from different kinds of plastic tubing. The whisky glasses are cut from transparent, eight-sided ballpoint pen tubes. The beer glasses are cut from clear plastic tubing. Make the beer effect by gluing strips of coloured cellophane inside the glasses and then glue bits of plastic foam on top.

The whisky bottles

Small perfume bottles filled with tea.

The bar

This is assembled from bits and pieces of cardboard painted brown. The brass foot rail is thin wooden dowelling painted gold and fixed to the bar with small screw-in eyelets.

The beer barrel

A rough shape is made from a toilet roll tube which is then covered with narrow strips of cork sheeting. Circles of cork are glued on for the ends and strips of narrow braid make the hoops. The barrel stand is also made from cork.

The door to the back room

This is framed in balsa wood. The velvet curtain is hung on a dowelling rod by means of curtain rings made out of circles of wire.

Bibliography and further reading

DISCOVERING COSTUME, Audrey Barfoot, *University of London Press*, London: *Dufour Editions*, Chester Springs, Pennsylvania

A HISTORY OF ENGLISH COSTUME, Iris Brooke, *Methuen*, London: *Hillary House*, New York

ENGLISH COSTUME, Dion Clayton Calthrop, *A and C Black*, London

FASHION, Mila Contini, *Hamlyn*, London

THE WEARING OF COSTUME, Ruth M. Green, *Pitman*, London

COSTUME, James Laver, *Batsford*, London: *Boston Book and Art Shop*, Boston

COSTUME, Margot Lister, *Herbert Jenkins*, London: *Plays Inc.*, Boston

HISTORICAL COSTUMES OF ENGLAND 1066–1968, Nora Bradfield, *Harrap*, London: *Barnes and Noble*, New York

TUTANKHAMEN, C Desroches Noblecourt, *The Connoisseur* and *Michael Joseph*, London: *Doubleday*, New York

DICTIONARY OF COSTUME, R Turner Wilcox, *Batsford*, London: *Scribner*, New York

ENGLISH COSTUME, Doreen Yarwood, *Batsford*, London

THE EVOLUTION OF FASHION, Pattern and Cut 1066–1930, Margot Hamilton Hill and Peter A Bucknell, *Batsford*, London: *Van Nostrand Reinhold*, New York

THE ROMAN IMPERIAL ARMY, Graham Webster, *A and C Black*, London: *Fund and Wagnalls*, New York

THE VIKING AGE, Paul B Chaillu, *John Murray*, London: *Cornell University Press*, USA

HANDBOOK OF ENGLISH COSTUME IN THE SEVENTEENTH CENTURY, C. Willett Cunnington and Phillis Cunnington, *Faber*, London: *Plays Inc*, Boston

THE COWBOY AND HIS HORSE, Sidney E Fletcher (out of print), *Grosset and Dunlap*

THE COWBOY ENCYCLOPEDIA, Bruce Grant, *Rand McNally*, New York

PICTORIAL HISTORY OF THE WILD WEST, James D Horan and Paul Sann, *Spring Books*, London: *Crown*, New York

THE COWBOY, Philip Ashton Rollins (out of print), *Scribner*, New York

RANCH LIFE AND THE HUNTING TRAIL, T. Roosevelt (out of print), *Fisher Unwin*, Reprinted by *Arno*, New York

OUTLINE OF ENGLISH COSTUME, Doreen Yarwood, *Batsford*, London

EVERYDAY COSTUME IN BRITAIN, Audrey Barfoot, *Batsford*, London

RURAL COSTUME Its Origin and Development in Western Europe and the British Isles, Alma Oakes and Margot Hamilton Hill, *Batsford*, London: *Van Nostrand Reinhold*, New York

Suppliers in Great Britain

Pipe cleaners

Tobacconists, Woolworth branches and department stores

Terylene wadding

Beckfoot Mill
Bingley
Yorkshire BD16 1AR

Department stores
Quarter of a yard makes approximately five figures

Wooden balls

The Needlewoman Shop
146 Regent Street
London W1

Hobby Horse
15–17 Langton Street
London SW10

Some DIY shops stock 25 mm (1 in.) diameter plain wooden balls without holes

Adhesive

UHU is available from art shops and stationers. The large size 00 includes a screw-on plastic nozzle for easy spreading

Sandpaper, wire, fuse wire and brass key chain

DIY shops

Items of general use eg pliers, metal snips, small hacksaws, etc

DIY shops, ironmongers and Woolworth branches

Leather and suede

The Leather Light Company
16 Soho Square
London W1

Poster and watercolour paints, felt-tip pens and coloured pencils, Plasticine, card, tracing paper

E J Arnold
Butterley Street
Leeds LS10 1AX

Dryad Ltd
Northgates
Leicester LE1 4QR

Margros, Artists Colourmen
Monument House
Monument Way
Woking
Surrey

Reeves and Sons Ltd
Lincoln Road
Enfield
Middlesex

George Rowney & Co Ltd
10/11 Percy Street
London W1

London showroom
51/52 Rathbone Place
London W1P 1AB

Winsor and Newton Ltd
Wealdstone
Harrow HA3 5RH
Middlesex and

Art shops

Plasticine may also be obtained direct from
Harbutt's Limited
Bathampton
Bath
Somerset

Sewing threads, wools, felt, needlecraft accessories

Fred Aldous Ltd
37 Lever Street
Manchester M60 1UX

E J Arnold
Butterley Street
Leeds LS10 1AX

Dryad Ltd
Northgates
Leicester LE1 4QR

The Needlewoman Shop
146 Regent Street
London W1

Nottingham Handcraft Company
Melton Road
West Bridgford
Nottingham

Felt may also be bought from
The Felt and Hessian Shop
34 Grenville Street
London EC4
Squares are usually obtainable from department stores

Sequins, beads, lace edging, shoe laces, braid, cord, ribbon

Department stores

Beads, sequins, pearls

Sesame Ventures
Greenham Hall
Wellington
Somerset

Enamel paints

Small tins are available from modelmaking and hobby shops

Ping-pong (table tennis) balls

Sports suppliers and toy shops

Fur fabric, buckram and lurex

Department stores

Suppliers in the USA

Pipe cleaners

Tobacconists, Woolworth branches and department stores

Terylene wadding

Department stores
Quarter of a yard makes approximately five figures

Wooden balls

DIY shops usually stock 1 in. diameter plain wooden balls without holes

Items of general use eg pliers, metal snips, small hacksaws, etc

DIY shops and Woolworth branches

Paints, felt-tip pens and coloured pencils, Plasterline, card, tracing paper

Arthur Brown and Bro. Inc
2 West 46 Street
New York NY 10036

A I Friedman Inc
25 West 45 Street
New York, NY 10036

Winsor and Newton Ltd
555 Winsor Drive
Secaucus
New Jersey 17194

Leather and suede

Aerolyn Fabrics Inc
380 Broadway (corner of White Street)
New York

Sewing threads, yarns, and needlecraft accessories

American Thread Corporation
90 Park Avenue
New York

Bucky King
Embroideries Unlimited
121 South Drive
Pittsburgh
Pennsylvania 15238

The Needle's Point Studio
1626 Macon Street
McLean
Virginia 22101

also from department stores